DBT WORKBOOK FOR ADULTS

A Practical Guide to Improving Mental with Dialectical Behavioral Therapy

Relove Psychology

FREE GIFT

Greetings!

First of all, we want to thank you for reading our books. We aim to create the very best books for our readers.

Now we invite you to join our exclusive list. As a subscriber, you will receive a free gift, weekly tips, free giveaways, discounts and so much more.

<u>All of this is 100% free with no strings attached!</u>

To claim your bonus simply head to the link below or scan the QR code below.

RELOVEPSYCHOLOGY

https://www.subscribepage.com/relovepsychology

CONTENTS

INTRODUCTION

Negative thoughts, disorders, and phobias can be exhausting to deal with, as they generate all kinds of difficult feelings—some are bad, some are good, and some are very bad or too good. Be what it may, they often become overwhelming, and it may seem like they are taking over one's life. That's where dialectical behavioral therapy steps in. Dialectical behavioral therapy is a type of therapy specifically aimed at making patients understand their feelings, accept them, and learn effective skills to manage them, giving them all the tools they need to make positive changes in their lives.

Dialectical Behavioral Therapy (DBT) can help people who feel hopeless, experience low self-esteem or feelings of self-hate and guilt, and people who have sudden and intense mood swings and often engage in risky or impulsive behaviors. Patients with suicidal thoughts (a tendency towards unstable relationships and self-harm) or who are constantly afflicted by powerlessness can also greatly benefit from it. The truth is, there is a wide and diverse range of mental health conditions that dialectical behavioral therapy can treat, from borderline personality disorder—which is its trademark—to suicidal ideation and behaviors, the actual motive behind its creation. That's an interesting story if you are curious. We will go over it in chapter one.

Depressive disorders, post-traumatic stress disorder, substance abuse, eating disorders, and even quite a bit of neurodiversity are all mental health conditions that dialectical behavioral therapy has proven effective to deal with. One-on-one sessions with a specialized therapist, well-rounded skill training modules done in groups, and in the moment phone coaching are the trademark DBT resources. With them, dialectical behavioral therapy is able to assist its patients on their journey to accepting who they are inside and out, concentrate in the present moment, find ways to get through difficult situations, and improve their interpersonal relationships.

Dialectical behavioral therapy usually lasts six months to a year and has a long and thorough history of success. As for this book, its mission is to provide an overview of the theory behind dialectical behavioral therapy, how it functions, the problems it can help with, how it can help with said problems, and give advice on strategies and exercises that one can start with as soon as they want.

Without further ado, let's get started.

CHAPTER 1

DIALECTICAL BEHAVIORAL THERAPY

Dialectical Behavioral Therapy, also known by its acronym DBT, is a type of talk therapy based on Cognitive Behavioral Therapy (CBT) that was modified to include elements of mindfulness. Dialectical behavioral therapy is an evidence-based method that mainly targets the patient's social and emotional issues, and is intended for people who experience extremely intense feelings. DBT helps patients to find ways to accept themselves, live in the moment, and develop healthy ways to cope with stress and other burdens (Schimelpfening, 2022). CBT, on the other hand, focuses on identifying a patient's unusual ways of thinking or on any psychological condition they may have (anxiety disorders or depression, for example), analyzes them, and organizes them so that the patient becomes able to curb their own troublesome thoughts and cultivate advantageous behavioral patterns.

CBT is a goal-oriented, short-term therapy based on self-awareness, while DBT is a long-term process based on self-reflection and personal progress. People who try and fail in CBT are known to thrive in DBT, as it is a more personal, customized approach.

Dialectical behavioral therapy focuses on helping people accept the reality of their lives and behaviors, as well as how to change them. The term dialectical, in fact, comes from the idea that bringing together two opposites in therapy (acceptance and change) brings better results than either of them alone (Dialectical Behavioural Therapy, n.d.). The end result of this kind of therapy is for the individual to recognize, accept, and process negative and unhealthy habits and emotions, especially during social situations.

But how does it all work? And for what, exactly? What's more, how did someone even come up with it? You must have many questions. Be what it may; don't fret. I have your answers.

The Story Behind Dialectical Behavioral Therapy

First things first, dialectical behavioral therapy was founded in the 1970s by psychologist Marsha Linehan, who at that time was a suicide researcher. This kind of therapy was originally developed in an effort to apply standard behavior therapy (CBT) to treat individuals showcasing extreme self-destructive tendencies. Dr. Linehan had personal experience with mental illness from her late teens and would have her research team call the hospitals in the area and ask them to send her their most severely suicidal and self-injuring patients. She would then try to cure them with behavioral therapy (Vaughan, 2022).

Now, it's important to note that most of the highly suicidal patients Dr. Linehan was working with met the diagnostic criteria for Borderline Personality Disorder (BPD), which she hadn't ever heard of before. She didn't know what it was or how to recognize it, and that was the root of the whole ordeal. Dr. Linehan had no idea what she was doing. She just wanted to help, and was willing to try anything and everything for the chance of making even the slightest difference in the lives of her patients, no matter how many tries it took. She was just studying suicide and trying her best (BorderlinerNotes, 2017a).

However, the standard behavior therapy of the '70s and early '80s consisted of the therapist being able to say, "alright, here is the problem, and this is what we are going to do to solve it," and the patient promptly agreeing to try that. But the people Dr. Linehan was working with didn't react well to this approach, believing they were being accused of being the problem. They often got upset and quit treatment, which caused severe adverse effects on their mental health (Vaughan, 2022).

Dr. Linehan quickly figured out that CBT wasn't going to work and branched out. She went back and forth between humanism (based on reflection and validation) and behavioristic (based on change) approaches. She first told herself that she would shift to an acceptance-based treatment and validate her patients as much as she could, and then try to guide them through changing their ways and improving themselves. The former resulted in the patients feeling like they weren't being helped, just listened to, leading to frustration and feelings of impotence, while the latter just doubled the belief that they were the ones with the issue and were being blamed for it. Neither of the approaches was effective in helping the patients, much less getting them "out of hell," which was Dr. Linehan's primary motivation (Vaughan, 2022).

So what happened then? Well, Dr. Linehan realized that she had to balance the two approaches. She had to encourage her patients to embrace their thoughts and emotions without judgment and without trying to change them, which would unironically allow change, as they would finally let go of the past and allow themselves to heal. Like this, problem-solving and validation became the core components of dialectical behavioral therapy.

All in all, the road to DBT was a trial and error process based on clinical experience and extensive research. But there is more. For one, what helped with this balancing of the different approaches was dialectics. Dr. Linehan stated that dialectics was a complex concept with roots in both philosophy and science—a process that involved several assumptions about the nature of reality, that everything is connected to everything else, for one. That change is constant and inevitable. And that opposites can and should be combined to reach a closer approximation to the truth, which is constantly evolving. (Linehan, 2020).

Dialectics is a pillar and guide for change, if you will: a contradiction between ideas that serves as the determining factor in their relationship, bringing forth a new understanding from their interaction. A middle ground where one can come to understand the reality of their situation while accepting their own biased feelings about it. For example, letting yourself cry because you failed a test while acknowledging that you could have studied more for it. When you do this, you allow yourself to work through your feelings and reflect on your life, taking an essential step towards true self-growth and happiness.

Apart from this concept of acceptance, Dr. Linehan made use of her Zen training (which now she's a master of) to apply Zen principles to her methods, introducing the elements of distress tolerance and mindful awareness into her developing therapy as well. This, she theorized, would be able to both lessen the extreme suffering of her patients and facilitate the changes necessary for them to build a life worth living. She was right. The first randomized clinical trial of DBT showed reduced rates of suicidal gestures, psychiatric hospitalizations, and treatment dropouts when compared to the usual treatment (Vaughan, 2022).

Dialectical Behavioral Therapy Today

Nowadays, DBT is known as the gold standard for treating Borderline Personality Disorders. In fact, according to Christian Stiglmayr and other collaborators, "at the end of the first treatment year, 77% of the patients no longer met the criteria for BPD diagnosis." (Stiglmayr et al., 2014). Indeed, while DBT cannot cure BPD, it is very effective in replacing maladaptive—also known as negative—coping mechanisms with beneficial ones. DBT is also famous for greatly improving suicidal thoughts and ideation.

That said, it would be disrespectful to suggest that DBT can only be used to treat BPD and suicidal tendencies. In fact, therapists often provide it for patients who present symptoms and behaviors associated with mood disorders and mental health conditions such as depression, Post-Traumatic Stress Disorder (PTSD), chemical dependency, and anxiety as well. A case study carried out by scientific researchers Regina Steil, Angelina Schneider, and Laura Schwartzkopff also suggests that

DBT is quite effective in treating sexual abuse survivors (Steil et al., 2021), and specialists suggest this therapy to be at least as good as CBT to treat eating disorders, particularly binge eating disorder and bulimia (Cowden, 2020).

But how? How can something created in such a specific way be applied to something else, especially when we are talking about illnesses and disorders? Well, the reason is that each of these other conditions is thought to be associated with issues resulting from unhealthy or problematic efforts to control intense negative feelings (anger, fear, anxiety, etc.) and/or physical or mental responses (flinching, spacing out, having flashbacks). This creates dysfunctional behavior patterns and a lack of balance, which in turn leads to overfocusing on one specific aspect of one's life, like work, relationships or hobbies, obsessive routines/rituals, hypervigilance, loss of self, constant exhaustion, and lack of drive. All things that easily contribute to a decline in mental health and emotional stability.

This is not to say these are the cause. Mental illnesses, in general, are thought to originate from a variety of genetic and environmental factors, like inherited traits from blood relatives, in which certain genes increase one's risk of developing one, and then a life situation may trigger it; environmental exposure before birth, like vulnerability to inflammatory conditions, toxins, alcohol or drugs while in the womb; and brain chemistry, as in, when the neurotransmitters in the brain are impaired, and their functions change or can't be performed (Mayo Clinic, 2019a). These factors are out of one's control, and there is little to be done about them apart from going to therapy before they even have a chance of becoming an issue.

However, there are risk factors that may increase the risk of developing a mental illness and are caused by our circumstances. These may include stressful situations, traumatic experiences, recurrent use of alcohol/recreational drugs, a childhood history of abuse and neglect, lack of a safety net (as in having few healthy relationships), and a previous mental illness. Like, what happens if someone grows up in a household where violence is the norm? There is constant screaming, smashing or breaking things, and actual physical, psychological, and emotional abuse happening all through their major developing years, plus a family history of anger issues. With a record like that, a person may start to hold back their feelings in an attempt to not imitate the aggressive tendencies they witness on a day-to-day basis. This, with time, will create a dam of repressed emotions that can badly impact their life.

For example, the patient will allow offenses against themself because they are afraid of confrontation, with the cause being the other person's reaction or their own; or they will start to believe that they are a fraud, a monster in disguise, and that they are tricking everyone who shows care for them. These things have an impact, and a heavy one at that. Ill-natured or imbalanced relationships with people have a bad influence on one's mindset and core beliefs; meanwhile, a bad perception of the self can lead to impostor syndrome (when someone believes they are not good enough for the people in their life between other things), self-isolation and resentment. And all of this combined? It could very well trigger the very violent tendencies the person was trying to avoid or other conditions just as bad. Worse, even.

So, need for therapy>decline of mental health>poor coping mechanisms>trigger>risk factors>genetic and environmental factors. A chain of unfortunate events whose weight only gets heavier and heavier with time.

That's where DBT steps in. See, DBT was literally designed to help people increase their emotional and cognitive regulation skills by learning the triggers that set off the negative emotions they feel. This therapy can help patients evaluate which coping skills to implement in different situations and identify the sequences of events, thoughts, feelings, and behaviors that cause these undesired reactions. It also helps cultivate relationships with the people in the lives of the patients, despite the troubles they may be facing.

The truth is any individual suffering from destructive behaviors and/or mental health complications can benefit from DBT.

Getting Started With Dialectical Behavioral Therapy

So how does the treatment work in dialectical behavioral therapy? Well, to begin with, DBT is a full program treatment with a multifaceted approach in order to address multiple needs at once; it teaches critical skills by exemplifying, telling stories, providing instructions, and giving feedback to patients, among other things. That said, there are three modes of standard outpatient therapy in which DBT can be performed; individual psychotherapy, group skills training, and in the moment coaching—outpatient, meaning there is no need for the person to stay in a hospital or any medical institution (What is Dialectical Behavior, n.d.).

Individual Psychotherapy

Individual psychotherapy usually involves around an hour of one-on-one sessions with a specialized doctor per week, for as long as the patient is in therapy, in which one talks about whatever they are working on or trying to manage. What happens here is that the therapist takes a close look at the patient's goals and figures out what behaviors they need to implement to advance their life towards said goals, helping them to stay motivated and, even more important, in the treatment.

Individual psychotherapy has seven areas of focus (Vaughan, 2022):

- Parasuicidal behaviors: Self-harm without the intent of actually dying.
- Therapy-interfering behaviors: Includes all things that get in the way of therapy, such as missing appointments and not talking about one's actual problems.
- Behaviors that interfere with quality of life: Like drug use, failure to take prescribed medication, and high-risk sexual behavior, among other things.

- Behavioral skills acquisition: Such as obtaining abilities that influence how one interacts with other people and the way that they respond to certain situations.
- Post-traumatic stress behaviors: Like flashbacks, nightmares, uncontrollable thoughts about the event, etc.
- Self-respecting behaviors: Meaning learning to love oneself and treat oneself with care.

These areas are supposed to supplement and add to group skills training, which will be explained in the next section.

Now, individual psychotherapy therapy serves two main functions in DBT; to enhance motivation and to structure one's environment. The former implies applying the skills taught in skill training to specific challenges and events in their lives, while the latter consists in successfully managing one's life in all environments, using the same dialectical, validating, and problem-solving strategies we discussed before to take back control of their life (What is Dialectical, n.d.).

Group Skills Training

Problematic behaviors have a habit of evolving as a way to face, or at least cope with, a difficult situation or seemingly unsolvable problem. From drinking in excess to smoking to overspending, these behaviors provide a temporary relief that is impossible to hold on to in the long-term. Nonetheless, the patients are doing this to cope, so DBT starts with the assumption that the patient is doing the best they can during their most trying times and sets on teaching new, positive habits to replace the negative ones. Skill training aims to enhance one's ability to manage themselves in all relevant contexts.

Skills training is often taught in groups during weekly sessions, with each one focused on a particular skill for an estimate of two hours. These sessions have a class-like organization rather than process group one. Patients get to learn from their peers' experiences in a controlled and safe environment, with available guides and therapists, which can be (and often is) exceedingly more motivating and inspirational than just having someone tell you what to do. The full skills training curriculum tends to take around twenty-four weeks to complete, and group leaders also assign homework and give their clients diary cards to help them practice the skills in their everyday lives. The former serves the purpose of reinforcing the skills, while the latter is usually intended for keeping track of the process and how they are using their developing abilities outside of the group. Patients are encouraged to talk about their diary cards with their individual therapists, but can also discuss them with the group if they want.

If it wasn't clear enough, it's important to clarify that each group member has their own individual therapist for additional support, who is in charge of personalizing the use of the aforementioned skills in different life situations. What's more, different schedules that teach only a subset of the skills or take fewer amounts of time can (and have been) developed for particular populations and settings as well. Neurodivergent people may not have the same curriculum as neurotypical people, for example, as the ways they process information are different. These are the benefits of such a personalized type of therapy.

Overall, group skills training it's a really cathartic and enjoyable process with guaranteed results.

Mindfulness

One of the most important benefits of DBT is learning mindfulness skills, which helps one to be fully aware of the present and live in the moment. This implies paying attention to both what is inside of them, like thoughts, feelings, impulses, etc., and what is outside, as in where they are, what they hear, and what they can see, among other things. It is all about the here and now; mindfulness skills are required to tune into the world around oneself and listen to it in a nonjudgmental way. This will not only help with dealing with stress better, as one will have an easier time slowing down and focusing on the correct coping mechanisms during hard times, but also on their journey of self-discovery.

See, when someone is not worrying about the past or the future, they have more time to find out who they are now: what they want and what they feel, and what lies behind their thoughts and emotions. And once one knows that, staying calm and avoiding engaging in automatic negative thought patterns and impulsive behaviors becomes much easier.

Now, there are two types of mindfulness skills: the what skills, the things one can do to cope, like observing, describing, and interacting with the world around themselves; and the how skills, the way one does the things they do to cope. These can be nonjudgmental, as in, with no judgment, but also one-mindfully (one thing at a time) and effectively (doing things in a way that works for the person doing it, regardless of expectations or previously taught methods).

All in all, the final goal of practicing mindfulness is to develop a wise mind that will help one keep their emotions leveled with their reality and stop overthinking.

Interpersonal Effectiveness

Interpersonal effectiveness skills aim to help the patient establish and sustain positive and respectful relationships with themselves and others, teaching them to be assertive while keeping interactions civil. Interpersonal effectiveness skills strengthen one's willpower to say no, express their own needs, listen and communicate effectively, set healthy boundaries, and deal with challenging situations, like telling your boss you want a raise or calling out the classmate that copied your homework.

Now, there are three main goals that interpersonal effectiveness skills aim to accomplish. The first one is objective effectiveness—getting what one wants in a respectful way, with straight priorities and balanced demands. The second one is connection effectiveness, which consists of improving and maintaining one's relationships. Finally, the name of the third one is self-respect effectiveness, and it is exactly what you think it is: cultivating self-respect (Mairanz, 2019).

Emotional Regulation

Emotion regulation allows the patient to navigate powerful feelings in a more effective way. A person that practices emotion regulation skills will be able to control their feelings instead of having their feelings control them, learning to identify, name, and change them by sheer will. To achieve this, one must practice mindfulness abilities first, as they will help with reality checking and self-acceptance.

The next step is learning opposite actions of behavior associated with specific emotions, so one can start doing the opposite of what your feelings tell them to do. Kind of hard to understand, isn't it? Allow me to explain: if you are feeling sad and want to withdraw from friends and family, then you should reach out to them and make plans to meet them. If you are angry and want to break something, then it's time to pet your cat or bake some bread. If you want to hide in your room forever, buried underneath your blankets, then get out of your house and get some sunlight on your skin.

Practicing the opposite of what one feels like doing during emotional distress is making an intentional choice to overcome gloom-ridden tendencies. One must always keep in mind that the exact moment that they become able to recognize and come to terms with their negative emotions, their emotional vulnerability is reduced, and positive emotional experiences are doubled. If one can control their emotions, one can change them. And if they can change them? Well, then there will be little that they can't do, won't there?

Distress Tolerance

Distress tolerance skills teach the patient how to tolerate pain in different situations. They consist of using positive coping mechanisms amidst the turmoil of emotional anguish and using several different techniques to handle it. Distracting yourself until the emotions pass by daydreaming, reciting something, or repeating an anchoring phrase in your head is one. Then there is also improving the moment or looking at the bright side (quite literally, both of them), which will keep the pain from becoming suffering and help one not to become bitter about the situation. Self-soothing, too, is effective and can be done through square breathing; hold your breath, breathe out, hold your breath again, and breathe in, all for four seconds each while visualizing your favorite place or people, planning an enjoyable activity, or fidgeting with soft clothing. Mentally listing the pros and cons of blowing up during the crisis is pretty effective as well. One more distress tolerance skill can be found in chapter five, "Post-Traumatic Stress Disorder."

Distress tolerance skills help one be ready for the moment when they have to face unpleasant feelings to either stay away from them until you are ready, or cope with them in a clean, healthy way.

In the Moment Coaching

In the moment coaching is all about the patient being helped in the moment they need it the most. This is done using phones and other types of live coaching, such as video calls and even text messages, for those clients who communicate better through written word. In the moment coaching seeks to provide in the moment support. The goal is to help clients on how to use their DBT skills to effectively cope with difficult situations that have arisen in the patient's everyday life, when they arise (What is Dialectical, n.d.).

You see, it's so easy to master the craft in a therapist's office or in a group of people who support you and understand you. However, the real challenge occurs in the outside world. The moment a coach is present, a person is never alone and provides patients with a lifeline to those they know and care about. This allows clients to call their personal therapist for guidance between sessions when they need help most.

Dialectical Behavioral Therapy Consultation Team

Well, remember when I said that there are three modules of dialectical behavioral therapy? That's not entirely right. See, there is actually a fourth module, except that it's not for patients. The dialectical behavioral therapy consultation team is the "therapy for the therapists:" a group of three to eight DBT providers composed of psychologists, social workers, counselors, and/or psychiatrists that work together in a collaborative effort to treat patients. These providers have a habit of meeting at least once a week to help one another manage the high-stress situations and potential burnout from treating high-risk patients. Consultation team members provide ongoing learning, support, and encouragement to each other in order to ensure their own mental health so they can keep helping patients despite the enormous clinical challenges they may face. Indeed, even therapists need support to stay effective.

It's important to clarify that being part of a consultation team is a requirement to provide dialectical behavioral therapy, as there is no better way of maintaining motivation (a key to delivering effective treatment), enhancing one's clinical skills, and monitoring fidelity to the treatment model, which just gets more and more complex behind the scenes. DBT consultation teams share information about their cases with each other to get external input, advice, and points of view. This information is not shared with anyone else outside of the teams and is handled with the utmost care, respect, and discretion. DBT consultation teams work as one: a solid, multifaceted unit whose very purpose is to provide balance, acceptance, and the tools necessary for change to their patients.

The Wise Mind Concept

As we mentioned when talking about mindfulness skills, a wise mind can help to keep one's emotions leveled with their reality, so they stop overthinking. But what exactly is a wise mind? And how can it be cultivated?

Well, Marsha Linehan describes the wise mind as "that part of each person that can know an experience truth (...)" (DBTSelfHelp, n.d.b). See, all minds have three different states: the reasonable mind, which shines when a person is able to approach a situation intellectually, planning and making decisions based on proof and facts; the emotional mind, which is the one that takes over when feelings are high and overwhelming, overtaking the reasonable mind with erratic and seemingly illogical thoughts and behaviors; and the wise mind, which is considered a balance between the other two, allowing people to recognize respect their feelings while acting up on them in a rational manner. (TherapistAid, 2015). A wise mind can be understood as that light-bulb moment when things finally fall into place.

Now, though it's difficult to find, everyone can access their wise mind. Stepping down from a situation, doing the right thing even though it's hard, or being able to feel calm after a bad fight or very stressful moment are all signs of a wise mind; proof that you have found a middle ground between rationality and emotionality. All that's left it's to hone that skill, and I'm about to teach you how to. Don't worry, it's quite easy.

First things first comes self-awareness: write down an experience that you have had with each state of mind this week. Think, how did you experience that moment? What were you thinking of? What did you do? Write it all down, watch the differences between them, and compare: with which state of mind did you feel best afterwards? (DBTSelfHelp, n.d.b.; TherapistAid, 2015).

And once you have done that once, don't stop. Take a few minutes of each day—or each hour, if you can—and ask yourself those same questions. It's very likely that you will start to notice a pattern, and even if you don't, at least you will have learnt something new about yourself and how well you are handling different situations (DBTSelfHelp, n.d.b).

CHAPTER 2
BORDERLINE PERSONALITY DISORDER

What is Borderline Personality Disorder?

Borderline Personality Disorder (BPD) is a mental health condition characterized by patients with extreme mood swings and problems controlling their emotions (Salters-Pedneault, 2021). BPD impacts the way the patient thinks and feels about themselves and others, which in turn affects their functioning in everyday life. It's an illness that affects the patient's self-image, goals, values, plans about the future, sexual identity, and even their likes and dislikes, all so frequently and so fast that it is hard for them to keep a sense of self. Indeed, lots of BPD patients have a distorted or unclear image of themselves, constantly feeling guilty and ashamed of the things they do, think, or say. They view things in extremes, either all good or all bad, so when they are called out for even the smallest mistake or wrongdoing, they are quick to convince themselves that everyone hates them, that they don't want them around, or/and that maybe it would be better if they didn't exist at all.

The truth is, any perceived act of rejection, possible abandonment, or feelings of disappointment towards a caregiver or lover can lead to impulsive and dangerous behaviors, such as episodes of reckless driving, fighting, gambling, substance use, binge eating, unsafe sexual activity, and/or self-harm (Cleveland Clinic, n.d.a). BPD patients may cut, burn or injure themselves—or repeatedly threaten to do so—if they feel like they are being neglected or left behind. They are also highly likely to have suicidal thoughts and can go as far as making actual preparations for their own demise.

BPD patients also tend to plunge themselves into intense, unstable, often very one-sided, and dependent relationships, as they need someone to keep them grounded and tell them they are loved and needed. BPD patients may also idealize people just to devalue them and believe that they are cruel and heartless when the person doesn't meet the standard that the patient set for them, or when they turn out to be different from what they imagined they would be. See, their very own unstable image of self makes it really hard for BPD patients to keep healthy personal relationships with others, as they can change their views of others as abruptly and dramatically as they do of themselves (Cleveland Clinic, n.d.a). So they may be all over someone one day, seemingly head over heels, and then it all seems to vanish the moment their partner or friends go off script and upset them. A burst of intense anger is repeatedly exhibited when this happens, which manifests itself in the form of biting sarcasm, bitterness, and/or angry tirades, making them feel guilty and ashamed again later on, effectively restarting the circle.

This, however, doesn't stop them from developing strong abandonment issues. BPD patients dislike being alone more than anything and can resort to extreme measures if they think they are being rejected, neglected, or abandoned, doing everything in their power to avoid both real and imagined separation. Tracking their loved ones' locations, for example, or taking over finances so they will depend on them. They may also go the opposite way and push people away before they can get too close, which can be very harmful to both parties. There is usually no in-between.

That said, signs and symptoms of BPS usually appear in the late teenage years or early adulthood, when one's personality is still developing and maturing. As a result, almost all people diagnosed with borderline personality disorder are above the age of eighteen, and although anyone can develop it, it is most common in people who already have a family story with it (Cleveland Clinic, n.d.a). Any troubling event or stressful situation would be able to trigger the symptoms, though having other mental health conditions can exponentially increase the chances of it arising. The good news is that there is a possibility that, with time, the disorder goes away completely, especially if it's being treated with therapy and medication.

Types of Borderline Personality Disorder

Discouraged Borderline Personality Disorder

Discouraged borderline personality disorder, also known as "high-functioning BPD" or "quiet BPD," is characterized by a mixture of avoidance and over-attachment to others. People with discouraged borderline personality disorder will commonly be seen following along in a group setting, showcasing both clingy and codependent behaviors (Guarnotta, 2022). They will seek approval from the people in their environment but also avoid them a lot due to feelings of shame, anger, and inadequacy, which more often than not turn into guilt, social anxiety, and even obsession. They have an extreme fear of abandonment, are easily unstabilized when faced with relationship issues, have a penchant for self-mutilation and other suicidal thoughts or actions, and showcase avoidant, vulnerable, and submissive behaviors.

Impulsive Borderline Personality Disorder

People with impulsive borderline personality disorder are usually thought of as unpredictable, charismatic, and overall exciting individuals to be around. They are very keen on attention-seeking behaviors and share the peculiarity of not thinking before taking action, constantly seeking thrills, and losing interest in what they are doing just as quickly as they started it. They show a mixture of melodramatic traits, like exaggerating situations and sharing unreliable but engaging tales about their lives, and antisocial ones, with these last ones showing in the form of intense feelings of irritability and annoyment towards other people with similar qualities (Guarnotta, 2022).

Impulsive borderlines tend to have very superficial relationships, short attention spans, recurrent feelings of rejection and fear, and a tendency towards substance abuse and self-injuring behaviors. They are very likely to do anything and everything in their power to receive praise, approval, and recognition from others, regardless of the people they may harm in the process—themselves included.

Petulant Borderline Personality Disorder

A petulant borderline is, in short terms, petulant. They are defiant, impatient, and passive-aggressive people who constantly feel jealous of other people's happiness and have anger outbursts in uncalled-for situations. These borderlines have a high tendency to come from abusive households where they were manipulated and mistreated by their supposed caretakers, which has led them to be wary of others in their adulthood (Guarnotta, 2022).

Indeed, petulant borderlines feel very insecure and are often cynical about their relationships, fearing that their friends and significant others may leave them, suspecting that they don't love them. As a result, these patients refuse to rely on their circles for anything, resorting to manipulation and controlling behaviors instead. They are pessimistic, stubborn, easily offended, and commonly share symptoms with depressive and paranoid personality disorders.

Self-Destructive Borderline Personality Disorders

Self-destructive borderlines are self-destructive. More often than not, they are their own worst enemies, sabotaging themselves due to a lack of a sense of self and intense feelings of self-loathing, bitterness, and anger. They are known to engage in self-harming behaviors with little regard for the consequences of their actions and desire independence, despite being deeply afraid of it.

People with a self-destructive borderline personality disorder also have a tendency to conform to other people's expectations, leaning towards sacrificial and risky behaviors and degrading sexual acts. This may cause them to feel resentful, frustrated, and unappreciated, which are common causes of self-harm, suicide attempts, substance abuse, and depression (Guarnotta, 2022).

Dialectical Behavioral Therapy For Borderline Personality Disorder

As we mentioned in the previous chapter, dialectical behavioral therapy is the gold standard for treating Borderline Personality Disorders (BPD). Extensive research proved that up to 77% of people with BPD no longer met the diagnostic criteria for it after one year of treatment with DBT (Stiglmayr et al., 2014). And while DBT cannot cure BPD, it is very effective in replacing negative coping mechanisms with beneficial ones.

See, the main struggle for BPD patients is to regulate their emotions, so the treatment for them revolves around learning to decrease and manage their feelings. Because of that, the abilities taught in Skill Training (as in chapter one, heading three) work together to target common symptoms of BPD, such as an unstable sense of self, dysfunctional relationships with others, fear of abandonment, and impulsiveness habitually showcased in self-injuring behaviors.

DBT teaches the BPD patient how to anticipate and recognize intense emotional episodes before they get out of control. Mindfulness what skills, for example, which teach the patient to live in the moment, target the patient's tendency to be driven by impulsive and emotional behaviors by instructing them in how to slow down and consciously engage in what is happening around them. Meanwhile, how skills have the intention of stopping the patient's tendencies to idealize or devalue themselves or other people, ruminate about the past, and worry about the future. This is done by training their ability to regard their present in a nonjudgmental way, with an open mind and kindness.

Also, many people with BPD have a history of childhood abuse, neglect, or other forms of invalidation that make it difficult for them to form stable connections with others early in life, which often results in getting invested in intense, unsafe relationships at an older age. BPD patients are known to have trouble asserting themselves, idealizing people and expecting too much from them, getting extremely upset when their expectations aren't met, and prematurely abandoning people "before they can abandon them" at the slightest sign of conflict. Interpersonal effectiveness skills help the patients communicate clearly to both keep their relationships and their self-respect; they teach them to ask for what they need and want, clear up misunderstandings, say no when they feel uncomfortable about something, and deal with the internal turmoil of guilt, stress, adrenaline, and relief, that doing all of this causes.

Emotional regulation serves the purpose of enhancing control over one's emotions. For borderline personality disorder patients, this means learning to identify and label their feelings so they can understand how they are ultimately affecting their overall functioning and pinpointing what is triggering those emotions in the first place. These triggers usually are dysfunctional behaviors that the patients have used to try to validate their experiences or get their points across to others.

For example, if you have a borderline personality disorder and are feeling rejected, you may heavily isolate yourself in an effort to get others to pay attention to you and include you. However, as people tend to have many things to worry about in their own lives, they may take a while to notice or think that you are just occupied, so they don't reach out. This would only worsen the way you feel, possibly turning despair into a rage and causing you to act harshly. Because of this, BPD patients are encouraged to avoid vulnerable situations that they suspect, or know as fact, that could lead to negative emotions and are taught to increase any and all circumstances that lead to natural, lasting positive emotions. Cuddling with one's pet may be one of these circumstances. Getting blackout drunk is not.

Lastly, distress tolerance skills will aid the patient in their journey to understand that accepting their situation does not mean that they must approve of it. Pain and distress are just an inevitable part of life, and not making amends with this fact will only lead to greater suffering.

Individual psychotherapy is also very important. As we just said, many people with BPD start therapy with an extensive traumatic history. In individual psychotherapy, it's the therapist's duty to address this trauma history once the patient seems ready to face it. This may include remembering the abuse suffered by validating memories that one may be doubting if they were real or not, and acknowledging long buried feelings related to the abuse, which are often the cause of seemingly unexplainable habits and reactions the patient has today. Reducing self-blame and stigmatization is another focus of this therapy, so the patient may free themselves from guilt and stop thinking they must do, speak, or act in a certain way to be worthy of what they want. Then there is also ending denial and intrusive thoughts regarding abuse, which means refusing to acknowledge the abuse happened or is happening, and sudden violent, despairing, or extremely anxious impulses, respectively.

Parasuicidal behaviors (which BPD patients often have), whether or not they have suicidal intent, are also never to be ignored in dialectical behavioral therapy. They are, in fact, explored in detail, putting special emphasis on developing problem-solving behaviors, engaging in active coping, and using short-term distress management techniques, though we will talk more about this in the next chapter.

Lastly, there is telephone consultation, also known as in the moment coaching. Patients with borderline personality disorder have a tendency to refrain from asking for help because they often feel invalidated when they do, resorting instead to self-harm as an outlet for their unpleasant feelings. At other times, they may ask others in an abusive manner or straight-up demand or manipulate them into cooperation, leaving people to feel used and wronged. Phone coaching is meant to aid with these dysfunctional behaviors by providing a lifeline for the patients, minimizing the reinforcement of parasuicidal behaviors, and encouraging them to seek help when they need it.

All in all, even though dialectical behavioral therapy is no longer the only treatment for Borderline Personality Disorder, it is still considered the best one. Dialectical behavioral therapy has been proven effective over and over again, successfully helping to reduce anger issues, suicidal behavior, psychiatric hospitalization, and interpersonal issues. Even the National Institute of Mental Health (NIMH) agrees that appropriate dialectical behavioral therapy for borderline personality disorder is able to help patients avoid developing additional coexisting chronic mental or physical health conditions, make healthier lifestyle choices, and improve general functioning and control (National Institute of Mental Health, 2017).

A person with BPD must, however, always seek treatment from a certified DBT therapist or psychologist, as care from untrained professionals is more likely to do more harm than good. More information about this can be found in chapter ten, "Finding a Therapist."

Write it Down and Let It Go

Patients with bipolar personality disorder struggle greatly with their overwhelming emotions, and a great way to relieve them is writing. You have probably heard this advice before, and you certainly scoffed at it, but it truly is helpful: writing down one's negative feelings on paper is a great way to de-stress. This doesn't have to be a neat little pastel pink note with the words "I'm feeling sad" in perfect cursive. No. I invite you to grab a black pen and the biggest piece of paper you can find and press down so hard into it that you rip it, if that's what you need. Beautiful, well-structured sentences are not necessary—you don't even need sentences at all! Words and even drawings will do, though the writing word will always help more to process feelings properly.

I invite you to let yourself go and pour your ugliest, nastiest, most resentful and hurtful feelings into paper and then absolutely destroy it, if that's what you need. I invite you to vent, to admit to all your wrongdoings, confess every sin, curse all the people you want… and then tear it all apart. Burn the pieces if you want, even, but get it all out of your chest, of your heart, and let it go for good. You don't necessarily have to rip or burn the paper, but it may be helpful in some cases, especially for the particularly bad things. Whether you keep it or not, however, the important part is not to allow the negative feelings to take root and drain you of everything that you love in life. So come on now, get your pencil, we are doing some emotional gardening today. Tell me, what thorny emotions are you trying to get through on this occasion?

And if it's still a little too difficult to start, here you have some pointers by Margarita Tartakovsky (Tartakovsky, 2016):

- Write about experiencing the feeling in third person, as it will put distance between you and the feeling and, with that, give you a better chance to process it without shame.
- Write about your memories. This one, Ms. Tarkovsky got it from author Susan. K. Perry, and I personally consider it one of the best. Basically, think of specific emotional high points throughout your life, and write about them. From the time you felt more afraid to the time you felt the angriest to the time you felt the saddest, write it all down, one paragraph for each feeling, and then develop each into a scene. It may help you untangle some trauma, it may help you cope with a current emotional dilemma—be what it may be, it will help.
- Give the emotion to a character. This is another way to distance yourself from the feeling: give the emotion that is overwhelming you to a character whose life, personality and circumstances are completely different from you, but who is feeling the exact same emotion. Describe them, their environment, what got them feeling that way, what will they do to healthy cope with it. It doesn't have to be realistic, happy or well written, it just has to be on the page and help you cope.
- Write about your feelings regularly, as many times as you can, as accurately as possible. Grab a notebook with enough space in it and write down the date, the feeling, the effect the feeling is having on you (Are you sad and want to withdraw from friends? Are you angry and in need to break things? Stressed

and considering dropping your work, or leaving it for tomorrow instead?), and what could be—or is, if you are sure—the cause of the feeling. This will help you notice patterns in the long term, from common causes between your negative feelings (people, a certain environment or habit, etc.) to things you can do to relieve them.

- Write about your emotions like you are writing a children's book, as in, with no complex words, simply and clearly, focusing only on the essentials to a point that even a little kid could understand. This method is particularly effective for people with busy schedules, as it is both very quick and very easy to do.

CHAPTER 3
SUICIDAL IDEATION AND BEHAVIORS

What are Suicidal Ideation and Behaviors?

Suicidal Ideation (SI) is a large and broad term used to describe contemplations, wishes, and preoccupations about ending one's life, which may or may not include a plan to do so. Not everyone who engages in suicidal ideation goes through with it, but if someone is known for it, it's better to keep an eye on them. However, suicidal people could prefer not to (or don't have many people to) talk about their intentions, so it's really important to be aware of the warning signs that indicate someone may be contemplating committing suicide. An unexpected change in behavior or the presence of entirely new behaviors are both major red flags, for example, especially if the occurrences start right after a painful or traumatic event, such as the loss of a relative/close friend or any case of assault.

These changes can manifest in many ways in suicidal people, such as previously nonexistent mood swings centered around depression, anxiety, irritability, or anger. Increasingly indulging in cigarettes, alcohol, or drugs should be worrying as well, just like withdrawing from activities they used to often participate in, self-isolating, and sleeping too much or too little. Visiting, calling, or texting people to get closure or clear things up and giving away their possessions or suddenly making very thoughtful gifts are more danger signs.

But suicidal people can be very vocal as well, especially if they are looking for support or someone to encourage them not to give up. One may not be able to provide a solution to a suicidal person's problems, and becoming their reason to live is unadvisable as well, but for these people, even the slightest show of care and kindness can mean the world. Offering someone a shoulder to cry on one day may make them want to live to see another, even if it's briefly. And regarding suicidal people, every single second counts.

Dialectical Behavioral Therapy for Suicidal Ideation and Behaviors

Dr. Marsha Linehan originally modified Cognitive Behavioral Therapy in order to help people with mental health disorders find lasting meaning in their lives, so they would want to stay alive even when they stepped out of the therapist's office. And she succeeded: DBT is, in fact, one of the relatively few Evidence-Based Practices (EBP) that has been found to be effective in reducing suicidal ideation and behaviors; very well-known as one of the most successful modalities used to work with individuals suffering from deep emotional pain (May et al., 2016). See, these individual mental disorders are characterized by high emotional reactivity and overwhelming or out of control patterns of thought and behavior. In addition, they are also at risk of Non-Suicidal Self Injury (NSSI), suicidal ideation, and suicidal attempts—all of which must be addressed and examined during therapy to determine where it's coming from. See, DBT is unlike any other approach, as it targets suicide instead directly of focusing on underlying disorders like BPD, depression, and PTSD. Dialectical behavioral therapy goes straight into assessing the factors that are causing or maintaining specific episodes of suicidal thoughts and behaviors, and goes to generate solutions to address such factors right there and then (DBT's Approach To, 2019). The four core skills taught in DBT have a leading role in this process again.

Mindfulness skills help develop a pause between feeling an extreme emotion and acting on an impulsive behavior (self-injury, for example). By developing awareness of the present moment, mindfulness aims to create a window of time between feeling and acting on that feeling in which the patient can reconsider what they are doing and implement a different copying mechanism instead. Detaching one's thoughts, feelings, and experiences from judgment is imperative for this to work, so it takes time and practice, but it is definitely possible to achieve and, by all means, beneficial. Furthermore, mindfulness skills feed into distress tolerance ones, as distress tolerance is yet another way for a patient to manage intense emotions without resorting to harming themselves.

In the case of interpersonal effectiveness skills (whose focus is on building one's personal intercommunication skills), they are meant to give the patient the means to express their needs instead of burying them, as people with suicidal behaviors often turn to self-harm because they feel like they don't have anyone to talk about what they are going through.

There is also emotional regulation; both the most important and the hardest skill to master. The purpose of emotional regulation is for the patient to understand that their emotions aren't permanent, and in fact, rather fleeting—that the highs and lows that their feelings experience, as well as the impulses that may come with them, can and should be controlled. This does not mean that the patient should become calm and level-headed all the time, as absolutely everyone has their bad days. No, emotional regulation just means not giving in to self-injury, despite what your mind is telling you.

Dialectical behavioral therapy professionals routinely conduct a suicide risk assessment on their patients in order to reduce suicide risk as well, mainly using an evidence-based approach known as LRAMP, or Linehan Risk Assessment Protocol, which (as the name suggests) was created by Dr. Linehan herself. This protocol includes a structured checklist used to assess, manage and document risk factors, comprehensively structuring a framework that describes the presentation, in session interventions, decision-making progress, and follow-up notes of a patient's mental health in a clear and easy to understand way for the other members of the DBT therapist team.

Suicide risk assessments must be performed when the patient starts with therapy and when clinically indicated during ongoing treatment (NSW Health, 2004). When a patient reports an increase in suicidal ideation, for example, or starts making plans and preparations to go through with it. However, there are also indirect indicators of suicide that a therapist must always be on the lookout for, such as access to lethal means, prolonged stress (especially if the patient is being bullied, in an unhealthy relationship, or unemployed at the time), or has been exposed to another's person suicide or over-graphic/sensationalized accounts of suicide. Historical factors are to be paid attention to as well: records of previous suicide attempts, for example, or a family history of suicide and childhood abuse, neglect, or trauma.

A proper therapist performing a suicide risk assessment will first identify the hazards or risk activities, then evaluate them, and then determine what precautions must be taken. Then they will record their findings in a risk assessment or management plan, which can be the LRAMP as well as any other, and frequently review their assessment. A patient's suicide risk can be assigned to one of the four broad risk categories; high-risk, medium risk, low risk, and no (foreseeable) risk (NSW Health, 2004).

Being assigned high-risk means that the patient will be relocated to an appropriately safe and secure environment, though not necessarily a medical facility. Assessments for high-risk patients are re-evaluated within twenty-four hours, all the while closing monitoring of the patient's mental health is monitored and properly handled. For medium risk, there is no reallocation, but the therapist must ensure that patients are evaluated again within a week of the initial assessment and go from there. That said, contingency plans are in place for rapid re-assessment if distress or symptoms escalate in both of these cases (NSW Health, 2004).

Monthly reviews are conducted in patients with low risk. However, if the low-risk assessment is determined after the person is discharged from an inpatient unit, the review must be performed within one week.

Also, said person ought to be provided with written information on twenty-four hour access to suitable clinical care. The assessment and management of suicide risk patients in DBT is conducted by a collaborative partnership between the person at risk of suicide, their therapy consultation team, their family, and the relevant health services (NSW Health, 2004).

Lastly, there is the no risk (at least not foreseeably) category; this is the one that belongs to patients who don't represent any current risk to themselves. Their suicidal thoughts and urges are still monitored, of course, as many patients can go for weeks and months with no suicidal thoughts, only for them to show their ugly heads again at a later point. However, this monitoring is usually done in the form of diary cards, the "homework" that we talked about in chapter one. Diary cards are papers, or an app, on which a person can record what skills they are using each day of the week, rate the different emotions they have been experiencing, and track target behavior usage (DBT's Approach To, 2019). Diary cards are meant to be filled out every day and also contain daily rates of urges to kill oneself.

That said, apart from monitoring through diary cards, high and medium risk patients are verbally inquired about their suicidal urges at the beginning of their sessions as well. This kind of routine monitoring is critical for the therapist's role in intervening when suicide impulses are getting out of control, and it also helps to keep track of the factors that cause their increases and decreases over time.

Furthermore, one of the main tenets of dialectical behavior therapy is to reduce the use of psychiatric hospitalizations, as there is no evidence that they reduce suicide risk and actually increase suicide risk in the long run. DBT is a form of treatment that takes into account that if a patient is in and out of a mental institution constantly, they are unlikely to have a reasonable quality of life because it is really difficult to find and keep a job, go to school, or even keep up with any type of relationship. Plus, mental hospitals are expensive, and the added financial strain doesn't do anyone any good. No, instead of that, DBT therapists provide skill-based, long-term solutions to their clients in order to reduce suicide risk while still remaining in their natural living environments (DBT's Approach To, 2019). Needless to say, these are the mindfulness, distress tolerance, interpersonal effectiveness, and emotion regulation skills that we went over before.

At the end of the day, the ultimate goal of dialectical behavioral therapy is to help clients build a life worth living—a life in which they can look forward to the next day, where suicide is no longer considered a viable or necessary option. Therapists must both identify what needs to change for the patient to want to live, and then help them to achieve those changes. This is where value-driven, short-term goals come to play. Simple things such as having a consistent and healthy sleep schedule, eating three times a day, and trying to clean once a week are all small pieces of the big puzzle that is a secure, enjoyable future. Everything is about small victories, about slowly and steadily building one's way to their goal. It is possible for highly suicidal people to build lives worth living, but it won't happen overnight, and it won't be a linear process either. But that is okay. As long as the patient is willing to try, everything is possible. And as a motivator, most people who receive DBT treatment show moderate to large reductions in self-harming behavior and suicidal ideation within the year of starting it.

Keep going, one foot before the other. It's not over yet.

Daily Card for Suicidal Ideation and Behaviors

As we mentioned before, daily cards work as a paper trail for one's progress throughout the day or week. A typical structure of a daily card will include two sections: one (usually the right one, as per the original one that Marsha Linehan shared in her workbook) which has boxes to rate emotions on a numerical scale as well as the urges to use target behaviors, such as mindfulness what skills, connection effectiveness or looking at the bright side; and another one, below, that contains a list of skills that one can check out according to their usage. Daily cards also often include columns to check off whether the behaviors were used or not.

Now, this all sounds quite confusing, doesn't it? That's understandable. Let's go step by step, and try to work out a daily card for suicidal ideation and behaviors.

First, let's keep in mind that the amazing thing about diary cards is that it's not necessary to stick to the traditional one. The important part it's in fact to find one that makes sense to the one using it—they can be customized, reworked and adjusted to everyone's individual preferences. Then, we get creative. We will start with something simple and useful, a base if you will.

Here are the instructions:

1. Get a pen, a pencil, or anything you can write with, and a piece of paper. An A4 paper sheet may work the best.
2. Now, draw something akin to a comparison chart. In the vertical column, write down the days of the week. In the horizontal one, let's go with the basics: write eat, sleep, and exercise/movement in one set, and then anger, anxiety, frustration, sadness, shame, joy, and powerlessness in another. This will serve as a way to track emotions and find out the correlations that self-care (or the lack of thereof) could have with them. For example, you may start to notice that you feel more angry or frustrated when you have had little sleep, or that you experience intense feelings of shame after staying in bed all day. For this, you only need to draw an X on the corresponding box.
3. With that down, add two extra vertical columns. For the first one, make it state "self-harm: A/U". A will signify action (as in, if you took action from that thought), meanwhile U will mean urge (if you felt the need to self-harm, but didn't go through with it). Then, leave the other blank, so you can add a number with a letter. For example, a day when you felt the urge to self-harm six times would read U first and six later.
4. If you are taking meds, you can also add another column reading "meds", and fill it with yes or no depending on if you

took them that day or not.

And that's it! You now have your very first daily card for suicidal ideation and behaviors. Try to fill it every day, and if possible, also keep a detailed record of what you do throughout the week. This daily card may help you pin down correlations between your routine, your feelings, and your actions, but a journal could tell you about further bad habits that you may be maintaining and that are affecting your overall health (DBTSelf Help, n.d.a).

CHAPTER 4
DEPRESSIVE DISORDER

What are Depressive Disorders?

Unfortunately, depression is a very common mental illness characterized by feelings of sadness, emptiness or irritability, a lack of interest in activities that were once pleasurable, and seemingly sudden changes in the way a person thinks, eats and behaves – eg worse

Depression may also cause difficulty concentrating, thinking, or remembering, and some physical symptoms as well, such as headaches, chronic pain, or other physical problems. What's more, many of these illness symptoms are very similar to those of suicidal ideation, as depressive people often have thoughts of death as well. Depression can be mild or really debilitating, and which form of it the patient is facing each day is entirely uncontrollable and almost always unpredictable. And though it commonly appears during the late teens to mid-twenties and often in women, the truth is that depression can occur at any time, to anyone.

Children and teens are no exceptions to this rule, though their depression can and usually manifests a little bit differently than in adults. Young children's symptoms of depression, for example, may include clinginess to parental figures, caretakers, and close family members; constant worry for their families and their own well-being; and aches and pains in the back, neck, and stomach. They may fear sleeping with stuffed animals because they think they are replacing their parents with them, which could somehow increase their chances of them getting into car crashes or dying in their sleep; or have a meltdown if whoever is supposed to pick them up shows up late, thinking that the worst has happened. They may even refuse to go to school, be underweight, or be overprotective of their families and belongings.

One should never forget that depressed children may seem more mature compared to others of the same age, but they are still children. If they are acting older than they should, something is wrong, as this can only be due to the fact that sadness and worry are weighing down on them and stopping them from enjoying their childhoods. No matter their attitude or their parents' understanding of life, children still need help, care, and nurturing, and failing to provide this will most likely worsen their symptoms. Never forget that at barely three years old, a child can already suffer from depression.

Regarding teens, their symptoms of depression may include sadness, irritability, and a constant feeling of negativity and worthlessness. It may involve poor performance in class, poor attendance at school, difficulty getting out of bed, feeling misunderstood and extremely sensitive, using recreational drugs or alcohol, eating or sleeping too much, self-harming, and losing interest in normal, previously enjoyable activities (Mayo Clinic, 2022c).

But what's the cause behind the depression? Well, there are several different factors that may play a role in it. Biochemical ones, for example, can affect the way the chemicals in the brain work and cause them to contribute to symptoms of depression instead of working against them. This is able to, with time and reinforcement, alter the structure and function of nerve cells or brain cells, further disrupting the way our most important organ processes information and assimilates experience. Genetics, too, have their own influence on depression, as the illness can very well run in families; there is a high chance that if first-degree relatives like parents, siblings, and even children have depression, then the patient may have it as well.

As for personality, it's very simple: having low self-esteem, trust issues, problem sharing, being easily overwhelmed by worry or nervousness, or being mostly pessimistic, all appear to be traits of people in danger of developing depressive disorders. What's more, long periods of stress, isolation, and major negative life events (the loss of a family member, a bad breakup, the disappearance of a pet, etc.) can't but aggravate these endangering personality aspects. One's history, though, is also relevant; a person's history of adversity (like being separated from parents at an early age, being abused or neglected, experiencing extreme poverty, having watched someone die or be killed, or struggling from youth with other serious illnesses) may also make them vulnerable to depression later in life, as it can kind of set the nervous system up for failure by causing it to overrespond to stress.

So yes, despite many misconceptions, being depressed or having depression is not just "being sad." It's not just about a "passing blue mood" or a "phase you are going to get through." Depression is not something that can be controlled at will or that will go away on its own. Work and care needs to be put into it. Luckily, depression is treatable, and one may be able to leave it behind entirely if they commit to trying their best during long-term talk therapies, taking their prescribed medication on time, or both.

Dialectical Behavioral Therapy for Depressive Disorders

Dialectical behavioral therapy has been shown to be very effective in treating many forms of emotional or behavioral challenges, depressive disorders included. This is of no surprise, as emotion regulation alone can make a significant difference in the lives of people whose very issue is managing their fluctuating feelings and irregular moods. After all, both of those circumstances can severely interfere with someone's daily functioning, provoking undesirable behaviors and situations and, as a result, causing negative consequences. It is due to these erratic feelings that depressed people may feel like they are worthless, which over time creates an unbearable sense of sadness that ends up looming over every aspect of their life; it consumes them with persistent, crippling feelings of unhappiness and hopelessness.

And while it is true that a combination of traditional talk therapy and medication works very well in improving symptoms of depression for most people, others could greatly benefit from a different approach. Dialectical behavioral therapy, for one, offers a comprehensive method focused on accepting uncomfortable thoughts and behaviors instead of fighting against them. DBT validates those thoughts and behaviors, making it easier for patients to change them. Positive reinforcement from the patient's therapist or support group (along with learning new life skills and coping mechanisms) can help one feel more motivated to change than they ever thought possible. They make a person want to push and fight for a life worth living.

It is this very core premise of validation and tolerance that makes DBT such an effective treatment for depression, as many depressed people are likely to be dismissed or blamed for their conditions. Whether someone who is suffering from a sudden lack of interest in activities they used to enjoy has started to show unprecedented signs of difficulty in understanding, concentrating, or remembering things, or is enduring physical manifestations of depression such as body aches, pains, and headaches, DBT can and will help them manage the symptoms, along with teaching them how to develop effective coping skills in case the issues raise again in the future. Can you guess what four skills can assist patients with their emotional dysregulation? You do know them, as we have discussed them before—they enable patients to gain a better understanding of what healthier feelings and responses should look like. Sounds familiar?

To start with, mindfulness skills—surprise, surprise—will teach the patient how to increase control over their own mind. For people experiencing the harsh symptoms of depression, this is a sharp weapon to wield. Once a patient starts training their mindfulness skills, they will begin to notice their thoughts and feelings in a nonjudgmental way, avoiding the unnecessary emotional distress that guilt often exerts over a person. Whether a patient has mild or severe symptoms of depression, reducing their exposure to pain and/or discomfort will be beneficial for them. Prolonged treatment with this approach is, in fact, guaranteed to reduce suffering and increase happiness, as it is a working effort to develop a clear mind and strong reasoning skills.

Also, there are times when symptoms of depression can cause a patient to act in ways that make the situation they are in worse. This is due to the fact that people with depression have a low distress tolerance, so naturally, developing distress tolerance skills is a critical part of treating symptoms of depression. Self-soothing, visualizing one's favorite place or people, planning an enjoyable activity, fidgeting with soft clothing, and mentally listing the pros and cons of blowing up during the crisis are all techniques that a depressive person can use to handle upsetting events and, with time, get to understand and modify their own negative thought patterns.

Additionally, negative interpersonal relationships and social interactions can make problems caused by depressive symptoms even worse. So interpersonal effectiveness skills, which offer strategies to reduce contributing factors to mood irregularities that surge during the patient's interactions with other people, are a must. They provide indispensable tools to prevent problems and resolve conflicts before they become overwhelming, tricky, and damaging to one, both, or all parties involved.

Lastly, emotion regulation, which we mentioned at the very beginning of the chapter, can help a patient deal with both mild and severe symptoms of depression by helping them properly identify an emotion and from where it is coming. This will help patients to manage, change, and accept said emotions. What's more, it could stop the paralyzing thoughts that frequently make one miss out on once pleasurable activities, feel helpless and controlled by their disorder, or act in ways they dislike and tend to come to regret. Emotional regulation skills will help a patient to better understand their feelings and empower them to stop them before they can even become a problem.

Diary cards play a major role in treating depression with dialectical behavioral therapy, as patients can use them to keep track of the invalidating thoughts and behaviors that affect them the most, as well as to record which coping mechanisms are proving effective and which aren't. Patients suffering from depression are encouraged to keep their diary cards with them at all times, almost like a journal, and bring them to therapy sessions so they can receive feedback from therapists and if they wish to share, other patients during group skill training.

In the moment coaching (or phone coaching), on the other hand, acts as a hands-on crisis intervention tool that can help one during an emergency. Like this—by making use of weekly individual sessions, phone coaching, and skill group training—DBT is able to help people achieve less frequent and intense symptoms of depression, boost their self-esteem, and stop self-harming, binge eating, and/or abusing substances. Dialectical behavioral therapy gets people one step closer to living their lives to the fullest. What's more, while DBT programs can last anywhere from six months to a full year, most people who participate in them state that they start noticing gradual improvements pretty early along the way. It is a commitment, and it is not easy, but all the effort will be worth it in the end.

Journaling

Following up the daily cards exercise and the write about your feelings regularly advice from chapter two, we reach journaling. Journaling is not much different from writing a diary. At its core, it's all about dumping all of your thoughts and feelings into paper to try to understand them better. It can also be done in an app or by voice recording, of course, but again, writing by hand it's best.

Many mental health experts recommend journaling because it can improve your mood and manage symptoms of depression. Studies support this, and suggest that journaling is good for your mental health and may also make therapy work better (Mayer Robinson, 2017).

What's more, journaling has been proven to help with physical health as well, lowering blood pressure, boosting your immune system, and improving liver function (McAdam, 2021). This activity will not cure your depression, but with only ten minutes a day it certainly will help you understand and cope with it better.

Journaling it's really easy because it doesn't need any techniques or complicated structures: you just have to write what you are feeling or experiencing There is no right or wrong way to do it—one day it can look just like a diary entry, while another it may be an account of what you did that day. You can fill a journal with lists of things that make you happy; with letters to your friends, family or that stranger that complimented your outfit on the street; with a poem, bits of a song that resonated with you or your goals for the future. You can use it to manifest, to vent, or to keep track of your activities. Be what it may be, journaling will provide you with meaningful insights of your life, making you more aware of your thought patterns and the inner workings of our mind. Believe me; sooner or later you will surprise yourself with your own words.

That said, here are some tips (that you make use of or not) to improve your journaling:

- Write at a time that it's convenient for you. Many people will tell you that it's better to journal in the morning, but there is no right time. I, for example, do it at night, and it's still working well. You can write in your journal several times a day, as things happen, or once at the end, middle or start of it. You can do it whenever you want, as long as you do it often enough.
- Don't force yourself to make it look pretty. Some people decorate their journals, adding pictures and colors and stickers to it. They write down their thoughts in an organized, aesthetically-pleasing way. You don't need to do any of that. You can be messy and disorganized. You can make spelling and grammar mistakes. You can write words wrong, be vulgar, and switch languages, pens and writing styles halfway to a

paragraph. It's your journal; no one else will ever read if you don't want them to.

- Don't be afraid to be honest. As we said before, it's your journal. Be honest about your feelings, actions, wants and intentions. You can throw the journal away or burn the pages later, but as you are writing, let it all out as it happened, how it happened, no matter how awful, embarrassing, or frustrating it may have been. What's more, don't hold your thoughts or actions over your own head. The past is the past—even if it happened a few hours ago, you were a different person then, so don't judge yourself.
- Don't be too negative. It's easy to let the bad thoughts and shame get to us, especially when we are feeling emotional, but don't let the negativity overpower everything else. I just said it, but I will repeat it: write what happened, how it happened. Be as objective as you can about it, to state facts, and then develop how the situation made you feel. If you write only negative things you will hurt yourself even more, and that's not what we are trying to accomplish here. You can write things that aren't positive, of course, but keep a balance, and even more important, be kind to yourself.
- Keep your journal close. You don't have to carry it with you everywhere, but try to keep your journal in a place where you can easily access it, and where you won't forget it. For example, you can leave it under your pillow or mattress, in a drawer near your bed, or in your school bag. Lock it if that's what it takes, but don't allow it to get dusty and go unused in your bookshelf.

CHAPTER 5

POST-TRAUMATIC STRESS DISORDER

What is Post Traumatic Stress Disorder?

Post-Traumatic Stress Disorder, or PTSD, is a psychiatric disorder and mental health condition that was caused by a shocking or terrifying (traumatic) event, series of events, or set of circumstances, whether they were personally experienced or witnessed (American Psychiatric Association, 2020). War, getting caught in a shooting, almost drowning, and being assaulted are among hundreds of other traumatic circumstances that can all cause PTSD. PTSD can be experienced as flashbacks, nightmares, and severe anxiety, as well as intense, disturbing, and uncontrollable thoughts about the events and feelings related to it that last long after it has ended. It can also occur in people from all backgrounds, of any ethnicity, nationality or culture, of any gender, and at any age, though women tend to be twice as likely as men to have PTSD, mostly from rape and sexual assault, intimate partner violence, and bullying (American Psychiatric Association, 2022b).

People with PTSD may avoid situations or people that remind them of the traumatic event; have strong negative reactions to something as ordinary as a loud noise, a particular smell, or an accidental touch; feel sadness, fear, or anger in unprovoked bursts; or act detached or estranged from other people, including friends, family and even lovers (American Psychiatric Association, 2022b).

However, not every person with PTSD has been through a dangerous event. Some experiences—such as the sudden and unexpected death of a loved one or having a special day ruined by someone else's ill intentions—can also cause PTSD (National Institute of Mental Health, n.d.b). What's more, though symptoms tend to begin early, during the first few nights or the first three months of the traumatic incident, sometimes they may take longer. As long as years, decades even. PTSD can be triggered by anything, even if the trauma was so long ago that one barely remembers it. For a person to be diagnosed with it, the symptoms must last a minimum of a month and be causing significant and continuous distress or problems in the individual's daily life. Also, post-traumatic stress disorder can last for as little as six months to a whole lifetime, regardless of how violent its nature may have been.

As for children and teens, they can have truly extreme reactions to trauma, but their symptoms may be vastly different from those of an adult. In children less than six years of age, for example, these may be wetting the bed even though they know how to use the toilet; forgetting how or finding themselves suddenly unable to talk; acting out, drawing or, enacting the event with toys; and being suddenly clingy with a parent or other caretakers (National Institute of Mental Health, n.d.b). Now, children with PTSD are at a higher risk of developing other mental health problems such as suicidal thoughts, depression, and anxiety—which we will discuss in chapter eight—so it's very important to get them the help they need as soon as possible before it scars them for life, or it gets worse (Posttraumatic Stress [PTDS] In Children, n.d.).

On the other hand, older children and teens are more likely to show symptoms like the first ones explained, more similar to an adult's, with the addition of unprecedented disruptive, disrespectful, or destructive behaviors; sudden changes in friends and interests; and newly acquired interest in drugs, alcohol, and parties, most of which are born from guilt (National Institute of Mental Health, n.d.b).

Indeed, this group is still made up of children, and one of the most common forms of an extreme reaction to trauma is to blame themselves for what happened, thinking they could have avoided injuries or deaths during terrorist attacks and natural disasters. If people important to them were affected or died during the traumatic event, the child may also grow up harboring deep feelings of resentment and have detailed, twisted, possibly endangering thoughts of revenge.

If one has persistent PTSD symptoms, it is crucial to find help ASAP. Dialectical behavioral therapy is a great option for that.

Dialectical Behavioral Therapy for Post-Traumatic Stress Disorder

Dialectical behavioral therapy is regarded as an effective, promising type of treatment for people who are in need of learning how to process and deal with a past traumatic event (Schimelpfening, 2022). The symptoms of post-traumatic stress disorder (PTSD) are challenging, to say the least; trouble concentrating and sleeping, vivid flashbacks, self-destructive behavior, difficulty managing emotions, and high-risk or impulsive behaviors due to intrusive thoughts and images are all serious issues born from complex trauma. What's more, the trauma itself it's horrible. From profound neglect to sexual or physical abuse to being trafficked, tortured, or held captive, or having been in an abusive relationship, it all results in deep emotional and psychological wounds.

When used to manage trauma, DBT is mostly focused on helping the patient handle their emotions in a healthy way and teaching them how to take care of their relationships with others, as it is familial, friendly, and romantic connections that are the most affected in the aftermath of a traumatic event. Dialectical behavioral therapy can help anyone with self-destructive behaviors that interfere with their ability to function on a day-to-day basis. If you haven't been skipping chapters, this may sound very familiar. Repetitive, even. The reason for that is that many people who have PTSD also have Borderline

Personality Disorder, which we discussed in chapter two, and both of these disorders are characterized by a certain extent of suicidal ideation and behaviors, which are inherently connected to depression disorders. That said, it's now time to introduce our four favorite techniques, now specially targeted toward symptoms of PTSD and extreme trauma.

To begin with, we have, of course, mindfulness skills, which are also known as "the ability to be fully present in the moment." Mindfulness skills can help a person suffering from PTSD to stop fixating on painful past experiences and/or future events that may or may not happen. Mindfulness skills are guaranteed to reduce dissociation—the feeling or intentional action of disconnecting from oneself and the surrounding world—and ground a person in their body. Regular mindfulness practice is perfect for increasing mental stability as well, as it makes the patient able to better recognize their ineffective behaviors and unstable emotions. An ability that truly can make all the difference in the future when facing stressors and coping with difficult times. Additionally, as the patient sharpens their mindfulness skills, they will start to realize that they are able to apply them before they even begin to spin out of control.

Indeed, as one gets better and better at focusing on their here and now, they will start to recognize their own stress-inducing behaviors and thought patterns—the ones that are, in fact, preventing PTSD patients from healing from their trauma.

Next, emotion regulation skills (managing, changing, and accepting different emotions without judgment so that they won't control one's life) aims to stop unwanted emotions from starting in the first place, working in tandem with mindfulness skills. See, dysregulated emotions are most likely a result of other PTSD symptoms in the first place. That's why DBT teaches the patient to accept and become comfortable with these unavoidable emotions, trying everything and anything to help effective behaviors become a habit.

As for distress tolerance skills (which we already know consist of learning how to tolerate seemingly unbearable emotions and situations and avoiding escalating behaviors), they are not different from those taught in the previous disorders. They stabilize and stop a patient from feeling overwhelmed. They help people cope with their feelings when they aren't sure of what exactly they want or are unaware of or what they need at the moment. However, up until now, we haven't mentioned the use of TIPP crisis survival skills (Greene, 2020).

- T stands for Temperature, as it is possible to be brought back down from a "feeling high" by suddenly changing one's body temperature. It's not unlike dumping cold water on a sleepy person's head to wake them up, really. See, if you wanted to practice this skill, you would have to dip your face in cold water and hold your breath for a minimum of thirty seconds. Doing this will trigger something known as the mammalian dive reflex, which can slow down our heart rate, decrease sweating, ease breathing, and even relieve chest pain. Ice packs also help if placed in the correct target areas, such as the base of your skull, your eyes, and the top of your cheeks. A cold shower or going for a walk during cold weather are great options as well. However, if you are looking to increase your heart rate—which may be the case if you are feeling depressed, sad, or anxious—then you need higher temperatures, not lower. In this case, take a long, hot bath, wrap yourself in a few blankets—the softer, the better—or drink something warm, preferably tea or hot chocolate.
- I stands for Intense exercise and consists of engaging in intense cardio or some type of aerobic exercise to de-escalate increasingly intense emotions. This is the step-by-step guide; first, on a scale from 0 to 100, write down your level of emotional intensity. Then exercise immediately, as much as you can. The usual minimum is around twenty minutes, but if you are unfamiliar or new to working out, don't exert yourself. Go for a walk, a jog, or a run. Swim if that's a possibility for you, or ride your bicycle, or roller skate. If none of that is an option

(maybe it's dark out, or you don't have enough time), do burpees, jumping jacks, push-ups, or high knees. Anything you can do in the moment, as soon as the problem arises. After exercising, rate emotions again. Can you see the difference?

- The first P stands for Paced breathing. Inhale for four seconds, then exhale for six. If that is too long for you, three to five also work. The final objective is to stop hyperventilating and slow down your heart rate, effectively reducing your breath intake to five or six breaths per minute. If you can, try to do the same thing as with exercise, and write down your level of emotional intensity before and after paced breathing.
- The second and final P stands for Paired muscle relaxation, and it means to, quite literally, relax your muscles. This one takes practice, as you have to clench your muscles and then unclench them, usually during paced breathing. When you inhale, you tense; and when you exhale, you relax your muscles. You have to concentrate and really pay attention to what you are doing and feel every muscle group as they follow your commands. Now, it's important to 1) practice before you are in a state of distress—otherwise, you may cause yourself a muscle cramp; 2) tell yourself to "relax" as you exhale and relax your muscles. This is where the "paired" comes from; you pair the word with the action in a Pavlovian-esque effort to, in the future, help yourself calm down more easily.

TIPP crisis survival skills aim to get the intensity of one's emotions under control in order to be able to use other coping skills. It's not necessary to do all of them, but it is recommended for those who have the time. TIPP skills are likely to ground a person for the rest of the day if done properly—and speaking of properly, a reminder; one should not overdo the activities from any of these steps. It shouldn't take a person more than thirty or forty minutes to do all of them. Any longer, and there is a risk of counterproductive effects.

Finally, interpersonal effectiveness for post-traumatic stress disorder steps in to guide the person through the process of being a good friend, family member and/or partner while maintaining healthy boundaries. PTSD makes it hard to trust others or be near them for prolonged amounts of time. Of course, this always depends on what type of trauma the person experienced, but it is frequently that a PTSD patient will need the tools to identify and let other people know what is and what is not okay to do or say to them and also learn to walk away from a situation if it's affecting them negatively. Exposure therapy may be an effective treatment for PTSD, but it must be done in a controlled and safe environment and never by unlicensed people, as well-meaning as they may be.

Dialectical behavioral therapy is able to offer support for all the symptoms that post-traumatic stress disorder may have and all situations it may cause. What's more, this support goes beyond individual therapy sessions and group skills training. As we well know, DBT offers in the moment phone coaching as well. If nothing else, it's at least worth a try.

Mindfulness Meditation for PTSD

Meditation is a practice that involves focusing or clearing your mind using a combination of mental and physical techniques (Cleveland Clinic, n.d.d). Meditation can induce you into a deep state of relaxation, reduce your anxiety, clear your mind, improve your awareness and reduce anxiety and stress, among other things such as increasing concentration and attention span and reducing memory loss (Cleveland Clinic, n.d.d.; Mayo Clinic, 2022a; LOiva, 2022).

Mindfulness meditation is a particularly effective type of meditation that PTSD patients can benefit from. Mindfulness meditation is not much different from the mindfulness concept that we have been talking about all this time: it's all about focusing on what you're thinking, sensing and feeling in the moment, without interpretation or judgment, narrowing your focus until there is nothing more than the present moment and you are grounded and at ease. This all will allow one to distance themselves from their traumatic memories and suffering, and look at the situation from another, more objective point of view, instead of giving in to the pain and hurt. Sounds good, doesn't it? Well, it is.

Here is an step by step guide in how to practice mindfulness meditation, provided by Emily Wise Miller (Wise Miller, 2015):

1. Get comfortable. Go to a room in your house where you won't be disturbed, and be at peace. This will not directly influence the meditation, but cleaning or tidying the space you are going to meditate in may help you to concentrate better, give you more confidence, and create a more lasting effect of relaxation after you are done. Remember, if you clean your space, you clear your mind.
2. Get in position. Sit cross legged on the floor with your knees wide, your shins crossed, each of your feet below the opposite knee, and vertically upright, with your shoulders and chest slightly forwards, and your hands resting palm-up on your knees, fingers loose; or sit in a chair, with your head and neck in line with your spine and pelvis, a straight back, and both your feet flat on the floor. Some people also practice meditation lying down, but beginners tend to fall asleep quickly if they attempt that. All in all, choose whatever position that suits you best.
3. Relax. Close your eyes and begin by taking a few deep, cleansing breaths. Breathe deeply through your nose for four seconds, hold your breath for another four, and then exhale through either your nose or mouth for four seconds again—whichever feels more comfortable to you. Wait another four minutes before starting again, and always let the breaths flow all the way down into your abdomen. It's good for beginners to set a timer for five minutes to practice this, since it can be hard to keep going for a long time when you are unused to the feeling of staying still in silence, breathing and doing nothing else.

4. Focus on your breath. Become aware of the sound, feeling and even taste of your breaths as you inhale and exhale. When you inhale, think that you are breathing in all the peaceful and joyful things around you, and as you exhale, picture yourself getting your mind and body rid of all the stress, pain and suffering that have been weighing down on you. Allow yourself to get lost in this moment, the world reduced to the rhythmic pattern of your own breathing.
5. Keep your thoughts in check. If you are just starting, it's very likely that your mind will wander, and that as a result, your breathing will become irregular. That's okay, it happens to everyone. You just have to realize that your thoughts have wandered and try again. If you only manage five minutes of concentration, that's good! A great start even. Time and practice will make perfect.
6. Commit yourself. Just like any other thing, meditation takes practice. It's not impossible, but it's not easy either. To make perfect you really have to sit down as often as you can and go through the motions. Even just five to ten minutes per day has been shown to make an enormous difference to well-being after just eight weeks of meditation practice (Wise Miller, 2015).

CHAPTER 6

SUBSTANCE USE DISORDER

What is Substance Use Disorder?

Substance use disorder, also called "substance abuse" or "drug addiction," is a complex condition that affects a person's brain and behaviors, making it almost impossible for them to control the use of substances such as alcohol, medicine, marijuana, and nicotine (cigarettes), despite the harmful consequences to their mental and physical health they may cause. Substance use disorder often starts with curiosity, with someone experimenting with the use of a recreational drug, thinking they will be able to control it, only to wake up one day, months later, and realize they cannot live without it anymore.

The risk of addiction and how fast it can happen depends on the drug, but whatever it is, it's guaranteed to lead to changes in one's brain structure. Substance use disorder affects the areas of the brain in charge of judgment, decision-making, learning, memory, and behavioral control, and it leads to changes in personality, abnormal body movements, and other behaviors such as stealing to get more drugs, lying in order to cover their tracks, and manipulating and shifting the blame for their actions on others (American Psychiatric Association, 2020). Some addicts may go as far as forging signatures and borrowing large amounts of money from suspicious people just for one more high. They also often become abusive, either verbally, emotionally, or physically, not because they are inherently bad people but because of the long-term influence of the substances in their system.

Reading this, one may wonder, why would anyone ever risk getting hooked in the first place? Or if it is so bad, why not quit? Well, going in order, people who continue to use—or abuse—substances after the first "experimenting" stage—which, to be fair, it's usually influenced by pressure from peers and a desire to "fit in" with others—usually do so because of other undiagnosed mental illnesses and the inability to cope with them. Undiagnosed depression, anxiety, or PTSD, for example, are really difficult to deal with without external help. However, instead of seeking professional help, some people start to self-medicate or use substances, relying on them to dull the pain and make them feel better.

And it works at the beginning. For a very short amount of time, but it works. Indeed, substances like drugs and alcohol tend to produce an intense feeling of pleasure, calmness, or euphoria in those consuming them. What's more, these substances are also able to increase someone's perception and senses, successfully improving their performance in once difficult tasks and enhancing their thinking abilities. It's the same thing that makes it so difficult to stop—it's good. People go from pain and suffering to constant struggles to happiness, joy, and productivity. Life suddenly seems full of chances, and it's like they have finally found the answer to their problems. Everything is going so great that even when they hear the horror stories of addicts that went too far, they convince themselves that it is never going to be them and that they can stop at any time they want.

But everything that goes up also goes down. The price addicts pay for these seemingly good effects (apart from the literal one, which is already quite high on its own) comes in the form of a myriad of physical, psychological, and interpersonal problems. They could experience seizures, suffer from strokes, become weakened or paralyzed, develop lung, heart and liver issues, lose function in their limbs, and drive themselves to an early death, whether from an overdose or a mixture of the aforementioned problems (Cleveland

Clinic, n.d.f.; Mayo Clinic, 2022b; National Institute of Drug Abuse, 2020). They also may develop schizophrenia, manic depression, and panic or antisocial personality disorders, among many others. And, as if that wasn't enough, they are very likely to lose a lot, if not all, the people they care about, from friends to spouses to kids to even parents and siblings, all driven away due to the danger to their well-being that having an addicted person in their lives represents.

What's more, most people build up a resistance to drugs the longer they use them, making them need more and more until they can't feel good at all without them, which means that it's even more difficult to let go. What if they are never happy again? And even if they tried to quit them, the effects we mentioned are very likely to last long after the immediate effects of whatever substance one is using wear off, causing withdrawal symptoms such as intense cravings, irritability, anxiety, sweating, and fatigue. It's because of this that substance use disorder cannot be treated at home, requiring professional help and continued support to stop.

Dialectical Behavioral Therapy for Substance Use Disorders

Once dialectical behavioral therapy was proven successful in treating suicide and non-suicidal self-injury (NSSI), Dr. Marsha Linehan and her team introduced modifications in the form of new principles, strategies, protocols, and modalities to target Substance Use Disorders (SUDs) as well, as it was considered—and still is—one of the greatest risk factors for fatal outcomes (Dialectical Behavior Therapy For, 2016). Dialectical Behavioral Therapy for Substance Use Disorders (DBT-SUD) aims to address the common problems and complications left in the wake of addiction, such as mood swings, social dysfunction, and lack of tolerance. Interestingly enough, the general strategies of DBT-SUD are much the same as those for suicide and NSSI; patients are in need of guidance regarding commitment, behavioral targeting, validation, and problem-solving. SUD patients are monitored on daily cards, go through urine toxicology screening, and are encouraged to participate in social networking meetings that support healthy attachments. What's more, their addictions are understood as a way to cope with challenging circumstances and experiences.

Dialectical behavioral therapy aims for an immediate and permanent cessation of substance abuse, but it also agrees that relapsing doesn't mean that the patient (or the therapy) can't achieve the desired result; it's just that it's hard, so the patient needs more support. So if a DBT-SUD patient were to relapse, they would be met with no judgment from either their therapist or their support group. They would receive more problem-solving coaching in order to reduce their risks of overdosing, infections, and other things.

DBT for alcohol and drug addiction, for example, approaches relapsing as a problem in need of a solution and treats that solution as something that can be found within the patient. Therapists walk their patients through the events that led them to relapse, so they can establish what exactly went wrong and when, and then help them to right the wrongs done to themselves and the people in their lives. This serves the purpose of increasing the individual's awareness of the negative consequences that alcohol and drug use have. They may be using these substances as emotional relief or as a way to numb their negative emotions, but that doesn't change the fact that it is a short-term solution for a long-term problem, and one that generates even more issues at that.

That said, in a typical dialectical fashion, DBT-SUD synthesizes the opposing main SUD approaches and brings them together by recognizing the wisdom and strengths of each one and using them to establish a solid commitment to abstinence, trusting that working with them together will bear better results than either of them alone (Dialectical Behavior Therapy For, 2016). These approaches are abstinence models, such as the Twelve Steps (a set of guiding principles in alcoholism recovery), and harm-reduction models like cognitive-behavioral relapse prevention (Hazelden Betty Ford Foundation,

2019),

Starting DBT-SUD, the therapist will ask the patient to commit to stopping the use of substances immediately. This doesn't necessarily have to be a lifetime commitment from the get-go. That's scary. That's a lot of time, strength, and effort. So the therapists may ask for just a few minutes, or a day, or a week if the patient seems to be doing good, possibly even a month. Any length of time that the patient deems acceptable will work, really. After all, this is an exercise done with the intention of having the patient renew this short-term oath over and over again, with intervals that get longer as time passes and the patient gets used to being clean. Processes like the Twelve Steps, or the Just for Today concept (a set of daily reflections and meditations meant to help people with drug addiction focus on sobriety one day at a time) both aim to achieve lifelong abstinence in small steps, moment by moment (Cuncic, 2022).

Then, as a harm-reduction model, there is the "cope ahead" strategy coined by Dr. Linehan herself (BorderlinerNotes, 2017b). With this strategy, the patient learns to anticipate potential cues of yet to happen, high-risk relapse situations days, hours, or at least moments before they have a chance to unravel. An additional technique able to complement and even boost the "cope ahead" strategy is the "burning bridges" skill, in which patients are encouraged to cut ties with their abusive past by going as far as getting a new telephone number, ceasing contact with substance using friends, and throwing out drug paraphernalia. Pipes of any type, for example—bongs, cigarette papers, cocaine freebase kits, and the like.

At its core, DBT-SUD promotes the belief that relapsing is but a part of the process—a slip that can be remedied and used as a learning experience and a way to establish better pathways towards abstinence in the future. The use of substances is disastrous and must be avoided as much as possible, but recovery is never linear, and it's the therapist's job to make sure to get their patients back on the right track.

It's also important to mention that when Dr. Linehan and her colleagues revamped DBT into DBT-SUD, many principles, protocols, and modalities were added. Attachment Strategies, for example, assign regular phone check-ins between patient and therapist to build a reliable relationship between them; develop social networks to help therapists reconnect with "lost" clients; and reinforce active participation in the treatment—as in, it encourages the patient to actively try to get better by sharing their problems and concerns with their therapist. These attachment strategies were added because many individuals with SUD seemed to be wary of commitment and tended to form minimal (if not non-existent) attachments to their therapists, which made it more difficult to help them.

Some other additional DBT-SUD skills include Community Reinforcement of abstinent behaviors, which aims to achieve abstinence by eliminating positive reinforcements of substance use and promoting positive reinforcement for sobriety instead. Then there is also Building Bridges, which is to establish secure relationships with oneself, the people in one's life, their superiors at work, and those they share healthy hobbies with so they may look back at the life they have built with their own two hands every time they consider giving in to their addictions, and take the deliberate choice of not doing it; and Adaptive Denial, which is a way to improve and maintain mental well-being by consciously (or subconsciously, once one has had enough practice) directing attention away from the stressful aspects of a situation, focusing on the rewarding and satisfying parts instead.

Another really interesting modality is Alternate Rebellion, a skill that involves engaging in new forms of rebellious glee that do not put the patient, their goals, or other people in harm's way. An example of Alternate Rebellion would be finally wearing the style of clothing that one wants, regardless of what people may think, or buying children's toys for one's own enjoyment despite being considered an adult. The point of this specific skill is to allow oneself to get comfortable in their own skin—to welcome all the innocent and small forms of joy there can be into one's life and have a good time no matter what others (or one's inner saboteur) say about it.

Over time, Dr. Linehan observed that the DBT-SUD skills were also very well suited and relevant for targeting many other problematic behaviors, such as "addictions" to food, NSSI, social media, and work, as well as others similar ones (Behavioral Tech, 2016).

How to Cope with the Cravings Caused by Substance Use Disorder

Substance abuse patients will often experience uncomfortable cravings (an intense desire to experience the positive effects of the substance they were addicted to) and urges (the impulse to satisfy said craving). These are the most common part of the addiction recovery process, and no matter whether you haven't used in weeks, months or years—maybe even decades—, you are likely to face them at some point. Cravings and urges are relentless, they come at your most vulnerable time, trying to convince you that you don't really want the changes you worked so hard to make; you need substances, you were better once and never again same. Drug cravings can quickly lead to relapse if not treated properly.

Drug cravings can be caused by a variety of reasons, from meeting or seeing people you once used drugs and alcohol with, to visiting places you frequented when you used said substances, to going through stressful or distressing situations that you used to cope with by using drugs or alcohol. Triggers can change over time and depending on stress levels and moods, so it can be helpful to use a journal to keep track of your cravings and the circumstances that led to them. This level of self-awareness can go far in helping you stay on track (Cirelli, 2022). Eating healthily, keeping busy, urge surfing (which we will talk about more in the next chapter), and practicing self care are all ways in which you can prepare yourself to fight urges and cravings (Cirelli, 2022; Tackett, 2023). Yes, it is possible, and yes, it has been done before, so keep going and don't lose your determination. I assure you, being clean will bring you much more joy than any substance ever could.

It's also important to remember that cravings always pass with time. They are not a constant, but a compulsion. Even the most intense craving and urges will subside if you wait for long enough—"long enough" usually being from ten to fifteen minutes, unless you are being exposed to the stimulus that cued the urge in the first place, in which case you need to remove it first. Having a plan for relapse prevention ready in case the worst happens is also a great idea (SMART Recovery, 2017).

With that said, here are five coping strategies developed by SMART Recovery that you can quickly benefit from, summarized with the easy-to-remember acronym DEADS—as in Combat Urges DEADS, each letter standing for a different useful approach:

- D stands for Delay, and it means to deny and urge over and over again, as many times as necessary. Once you have denied an urge, you know you can do it, and once you know you can trust yourself to do it, it becomes much easier. You will notice that after a short time, there will be fewer cravings, and that the ones you have will diminish in intensity. Waiting them out is a great step to recovery.
- E stands for Escape. Indeed, there is no shame in leaving or getting away from the urge provoking situation. Run away from it, and don't look back. Leave the pub so that you can stop staring at the beer taps, don't visit friends who smoke inside their homes, leave the supermarket immediately if you notice yourself getting tempted by all the bottles of wine that are so nicely displayed. Do whatever you have to do, and don't feel bad for it. If there's an alcohol ad on TV, switch the channel. If someone offers you a joint, turn them down. Just the act of escaping the trigger will focus your mind on something new–which will quickly lessen the urge. What's more, the pride you will feel for standing your ground will greatly fuel your recovery process.

- A stands for Accept, as in, putting your urges and cravings into perspective by understanding that they are normal and will pass. They are just another part of the process, and as long as you don't give in to them, you are fine. And even if you do give in, you can just start over. This is a long term process, and you get as many tries at it as you are willing to give it.
- D stands for Dispute: disputing the thoughts that are causing the urge or craving, and talking yourself out of giving in using logic and reason. And because urges and cravings often cloud your mind and prevent you from seeing the big picture outside the immediate moment, already having a list containing all the reasons that you've chosen to quit in the first place as well as all of the negative consequences that could occur if you choose to use it is a great way to do this (Tackett, 2023). Keep the list in your pockets, purse, or stored in your phone case. Anywhere where it is easily and quickly accessible.
- S stands for Substitute. There are many wants in which you can substitute an urge or craving. Take a walk, engage in a sport, or any other form of exercise. Pick up something new to read or turn on something to listen to. Start learning a new language or pick up a new hobby, such as painting, gardening, writing or meditating. Anything that can distract your mind and body from the urge or craving is good, as long as it's healthy and doesn't disrupt your daily life.

You can easily incorporate Combat Urges DEADS to your distress tolerance skills, and refine them until they come to you as naturally as writing or reading. So keep your chin up and your resolve firm, the battle is not over yet!

CHAPTER 7
EATING DISORDER

What Are Eating Disorders?

Eating disorders are serious and gravely endangering conditions characterized by detrimental eating behaviors that are associated with distressing thoughts and feelings. There are no known causes for eating disorders. They have a tendency to further impact the patient's health, emotions, and abilities to function (all psychological, social, and physical of them). Negatively, of course.

There are many types of eating disorders, from anorexia nervosa (an illness distinguished by an abnormally low body weight paired up with an intense fear of gaining weight and a distorted perfection of it) to Avoidant Restrictive Food Intake Disorder (also known as "ARFID," a condition similar to anorexia in which a person avoids eating certain foods or types of food and has a limited food consumption), to pica (an eating disorder that leads a person to eat things that aren't food, like dirt, clay or paper) to many more. The thing is, all of them are related, in one way or another, to issues with one's weight, body shape, and food consumption. They all share the trait of being very, very harmful to one's health, impacting their heart, digestive system, skin, bones, joints, and energy levels, always badly.

It's important to clarify, however, that though they are most common in women in their teens and young adult years, specifically from ages twelve to thirty-five, eating disorders can occur at any age and affect any gender.

In this chapter, we are going to go over two types of eating disorders in particular; binge eating disorder and what's known as "bulimia nervosa."

Binge eating disorder is a severe and life-threatening type of eating disorder in which patients present a tendency to consume unusually large amounts of food very quickly, sometimes to the point of discomfort and pain, and seem to be unable to stop eating. Patients report losing control of what they are doing as they binge, being unable to stop even when they want to, and experiencing feelings of extreme shame, distress, and guilt afterwards. To be clear, binge eating has not a single thing to do with "overindulging" in food or "having an enormous appetite": this is an illness, and people suffer from it on a daily basis. Some can't even remember what exactly they ate, as there is a level of dissociation from the patient's experience.

Eating distressing amounts of food faster than normal until one's uncomfortably full and possibly even nauseous, usually despite not feeling hungry, are some of the most common symptoms of a binge eating disorder. Patients also tend to feel disgusted with themselves, embarrassed and depressed after coming back to their senses, fear eating out with others and feel uncomfortable while doing so, and show extreme concern about their body's weight and shape. This, however, doesn't stop them from stealing and hoarding food and scheduling binge sessions—they can, in fact, go as far as eating food that has been thrown away. What's more, binge eating usually happens in private, where patients won't be seen or easily stopped. Indeed, while patients often hate themselves for their actions later, urges that are left unchecked easily become impossible to deny; feeling anxious, upset, afraid, and even angry can all lead patients to give in to the pull.

Patients with a binge eating disorder can often be seen starting all kinds of diets as well, which, more often than not, leads to even more binge eating due to both hunger and cravings. Episodes of binge eating usually happen at least once a week for a minimum period of three months before a person is diagnosed with a binge eating disorder. And being diagnosed is important since binge eating persists for years and years, and the complications it generates can be disastrous. Kidney failure is one of the most common, but high blood pressure, heart problems, strokes, and death are not too far behind. Seeking help is imperative. The good thing is you are about to learn where to start.

But first—or not, you may skip to the next part if you want—bulimia nervosa. Bulimia nervosa is, too, an eating disorder known for overeating or binging, different from an actual binge eating disorder because of the fact that following their binging episodes, bulimia patients engage in all kinds of unadvisable compensatory behaviors in an effort to eliminate the extra calories they have ingested. These compensatory behaviors range from purging (the abrupt and often even violent act of getting rid of the consumed food, usually by inducing vomit), unhealthily long periods of fasting, enemas, possibly endangering uses of laxatives and diuretics (water pills that, in this case, are likely to be misused to cause diarrhea or nausea), and compulsive exercising.

Some of the most notorious signs of bulimia are dental problems, inflamed or sore throats, irregular or absent periods, dizzy spells with not-so-occasional fainting, constant tiredness and notable decreases in energy, a persistent feeling of being cold, sleep problems, bloodshot eyes, among many, many others. The problem is that all of those can be symptoms of many things, and as bulimia patients tend to keep a normal body weight with the intention of not getting caught, the illness can be very difficult to identify. Many patients are, in fact, never found out, and since bulimia is treatable but doesn't go away on its own, they can reach the age of thirty or fifty and still have it. By then, however, it will be much more difficult to treat, as the negative habits and behaviors have already been deeply ingrained in their routines, making them really hard to change. But hard doesn't mean impossible, and as long as the patient is willing to try, hope is not to be lost.

Dialectical Behavioral Therapy for Eating Disorders

As we mentioned at the end of chapter six, it didn't take Dr.

Linehan too long to realize that the DBT-SUD skills were very well suited for targeting other problematic behaviors, one of these being "addictions" to food, also known as Eating Disorders (EDs). As we know, various eating disorder behaviors (binge eating, purging, etc.) are caused by negative mood states, like sadness, loneliness, frustration, and anger, among others. This is what allowed Dr. Linehan and her team to connect the dots and realize that the function of eating disorder behaviors in EDs patients was the same as the function of self-injuring behaviors in BPD patients—an escape from unpleasant emotions, thoughts, and situations (Cowden, 2020). It's the same reason why DBT qualifies as a good option to teach patients how to regulate and manage their feelings.

By adapting DBT a little, Dr. Linehan's Skills Training Manual for Treating Borderline Personality Disorder proved this therapy to be an effective treatment for both slowing down and straight-up, stopping problematic behaviors in eating disorders. However, these results were obtained from patients with Binge Eating Disorder (BED) and bulimia nervosa only (Cowden, 2020). There is no proof backing up success with anorexia nervosa or any other type of eating disorder. That said, this second group may be interested in Cognitive Behavioral Therapy instead, which is actually considered the first line of treatment for EDs.

Anyhow, dialectical behavioral therapy is a great option for people who haven't been able to make improvements with CBT or other individual psychotherapies. DBT for eating disorders is more costly and long-term than CBT, but also an extremely personalized approach that provides intensive and in the moment care, and has specialized techniques different from those used for BPD. Mindful eating, for example, which is a person's ability to focus on their eating experience; a focus on body-related sensations like taste and smell; self-awareness of one's thoughts and feelings about the food they are consuming; and urge surfing, which is a technique that can be used to avoid acting on any behavior that the patient may want, or need, to reduce or stop.

See, urge surfing can be used to fight any type of craving, from smoking to fighting to—you guessed it—eating. See, not unlike actual waves, urges peak and lose force, usually in less than 30 minutes. So, just as the name suggests, urge surfing encourages the patient to stop both padding (fighting the urge) and letting themselves be thrown under (giving into the urge); it consists of learning to notice the urges and then letting them pass without response; keeping in mind that it's just a craving, a momentary need. It will go away if given enough time.

Then there is dialectical abstinence as well, considered essential for BED treatment. We talked about it in chapter one, but dialectical is defined as something that concerns two opposing factors (Dialectical, n.d.). In binge-eating disorders, these forces are thought to be the need for the patient to keep a food plan that lacks triggering food (triggering food being chocolate, chips, ice cream, and the like; anything able to kick-start the need to eat more) and the fact that doing that seems to be virtually impossible for freshly started patients. Following a food plan is not easy for anyone, much less for people with actual eating disorders. And it just gets harder and harder the more you think about it; if one tries to perfectly follow a food plan, it takes the smallest slip to have a major fallback and be back on step one, this time with the remnants of one's confidence lying in tatters on the ground.

For example, let's say that you vow to yourself to stop eating chocolate for good and do stop for around three weeks. Then, one day, a friend of yours gifts you chocolate. Maybe it's Valentine's Day; maybe it's your birthday; maybe they just felt in a giving mood. The thing is, now you have chocolate in your hand, and it's relatively small, and it was a gift. You think I can allow myself this, just this one time, or, It's no big deal. You convince yourself that eating the small chocolate counts as a reward and that you won't do it again. So you eat the chocolate. And then you finished the chocolate, and it was very good, just like you remembered. You want more, and you have been doing so well, so the momentary cheat becomes a cheat day. And since it's only one day, you have to make the most of it. So you buy a ton of chocolate, and eat until you feel sick. And then, of course, there is leftover chocolate the next day, and without you realizing it, the cheat day becomes days, and then weeks, and then you realize you have failed to reach your goal for good.

This last realization is likely to make a patient believe they are unable to actually change, and so they continue to engage in their problematic behavior until they are either stopped by health concerns or shamed into trying again. Now, with sticking to a food plan discarded, another approach would be to just accept that having slips is inevitable, and embrace that fact. However, this doesn't solve anything. Slipping will quickly become the norm, and no progress or difference will be made.

So what can one do? What possible solution could dialectical behavioral therapy provide for this ordeal? Well, the trick is in the name. Dialectical does mean something that concerns two opposing forces, but it also stands for the fact that bringing these two opposites together and balancing them is what will finally bring results (Dialectical, n.d.). In the case of a binge eating disorder, slipping will happen, and there is little one can do about it apart from letting that frustration go and just starting again. Start over immediately. You ate all the chocolate yesterday—throw away the leftovers! Give them to your neighbor, the people walking past your street, or a homeless person! You may have failed this time, but the next one may be the one, so keep trying.

But not to forget, part of the specialized techniques that DBT uses to target binge eating does include developing an individualized food plan that will support the patient's goals and nutritional needs (Carmel, n.d.). Even if they don't follow it down to the detail, sticking to as much as possible for as long as they are able will inevitably make it into their lifestyle, not just their guideline. Change doesn't happen in a straight line but in a continued one. The solution is to not let go of the pen.

As for bulimia nervosa, it all starts by targeting the root of the problem, which dialectical behavioral therapy identifies as emotional dysregulation. With the core problem clear, DBT sets on teaching patients the correct skills (which we well know; our darling four) to deal with said emotions, guiding them through the journey to fix their dysfunctional behaviors. Results show that the binge eating and purging habits of bulimia patients suffer a significant decrease after receiving proper treatment. Mindfulness skills will increase awareness in order to fight back the dissociation tendencies of many binge eaters. Emotional regulation skills will help them navigate troubling emotions and cravings, while distress tolerance skills stop them from giving in and engaging in harmful eating coping behaviors. Furthermore, interpersonal effectiveness skills will aid the patient in coming up with on the spot, concrete solutions to any possible problem they may find themselves in, and the conversational ability to stop others from putting their newfound values and needs in doubt.

When applied to eating disorders, dialectical behavioral therapy sessions are centered on skills group training for binge eating disorder and individual psychotherapy for bulimia nervosa.

Say Thank You

Individuals who have previously shown weight concerns and a preoccupation with weight, have a history of dieting, and display a negative body image all show risk factors for developing eating disorders (McCallum Place Eating Disorder Center, 2023). In a society like ours, where we are being bombarded with messages of the thin and fit ideal from all sides—from movies, to TV Shows, to music videos and all kinds of influences, comics, video games, etc.—, it's quite easy to forget that weight does not equate beauty, nor health, nor worth. It's quite easy to forget that our bodies are much more than their reflection in the mirror, and all the amazing things they do for us.

Every day, it's our bodies that are keeping us alive. They pump the blood running through our veins and the air we use to breathe. They produce the energy we need to walk and imagine and do our favorite activities, such as dancing or playing an instrument or doing math—

and yes, there are people who do math for fun. Think about it, don't your legs take you to all your favorite places? Aren't those the arms you use to hug the people you love? They are! Your waist may not be the smallest and your stomach may not be the firmest, but really, is it so important? The people worth having in your life won't require you to be fit or slim to treat you well, and as long as you can enjoy the things that make you happy, isn't that all that matters? If you can hold people close, pet cats in the street, make silly dances with your friends and sing when you shower, does it really matter if you can fit in the pants you bought half a decade ago?

You may not be ready to read it yet, much less to accept it, but it isn't. Your body is capable of many amazing things, and it does them every day so you can enjoy hot drinks in winter and the satisfying crunch of leaves under your boots in autumn; so you can feel the nice breezes of spring against your face and the warm sun of summer in your skin. So sit down with a pen or a paper and ask yourself, when was the last time that your body had your back? Maybe you catched your balance at the perfect time so you didn't fall, maybe you remembered an important detail on a test (Raymond, n.d.). Be what it may, didn't you feel grateful then? Proud? Happy? Weren't you relieved? Didn't you feel so light and bright and warm that you couldn't help but smile? You probably did, so make a list.

Make a list, write a paragraph, write a letter even, if you want. Write something to say thank you to your body for the things it has given you, like you would thank a friend, family member or anyone you love. Even if it feels superficial at first, or shallow; even if it feels egocentric, note down all the little things you can thank your body for, and then all the things you like about it. Can't think of anything? Let me give you a few examples. You could be thankful for…

- The eyes that you use to read your comfort books or watch your favorite movie;
- That time when you were laughing so hard your stomach hurt and you could barely breathe, and yet you pulled through;

- The mannerisms that you got from your loved ones.

There are many things to love about your body. You only have to actually sit down and think of them. And once you have thought of them, write them down so you can remember them next time you feel down.

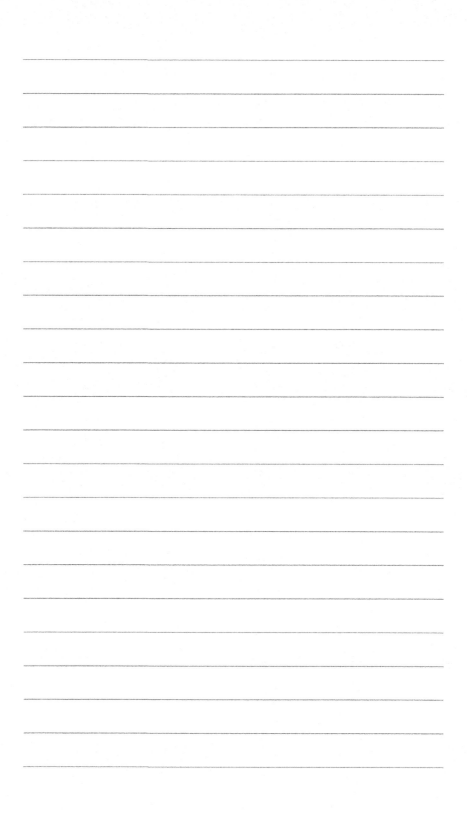

CHAPTER 8
NEURODIVERSITY

What is Neurodiversity?

Neurodiversity is a concept related to the range of differences in brain functions and behavioral traits that neurodivergent people have. In turn, neurodivergent is a nonmedical term used to describe individuals whose brains process, learn, and behave differently from what's considered the standard, directly opposing the concept of neurotypical (What Is It Really, 2023). As such, neurotypical is the way one can refer to people whose strengths and challenges aren't affected by developments that change how their brains work—people who have a "typical" neurological development. Is it confusing? Let me make it simple: neurodivergent people "differ" from the norm in the way they approach and view life, while neurotypical people do not.

On the one hand, neurodivergent people tend to have better memory; can intensely focus on a specific topic of their interest; exhibit strong abilities with systems, like computer programming, math, music, and arts; are very creative and detail-oriented; have a good long-term memory and observational skills; and can often solve complex problems with ease. Of course, not all neurodivergent people can do all of this, and not everything that comes with neurodivergence is positive, but there is no doubt that these kinds of people deserve the same respect and opportunities as neurotypical people.

See, neurodivergence is not a disorder, a problem, nor an abnormality of any kind. Some disorders may fall under its umbrella, yes, and many neurodivergence are considered disabilities, but that doesn't mean that's the core of the matter—it doesn't mean they are bad. Neurodivergence is just a state of nature like any other, a different and unique way of interacting with the world. In fact, neurodivergence is only considered a disability because of how inaccessible our society is for people who have them.

Neurodiversity embraces all differences, from medical disorders to learning disabilities and many more conditions. It views correctly that both brain functions and behavioral traits are nothing more than simple indicators of how diverse and unique the human race is. What's more, though neurotypical people tend to think that there is one correct way to do things (the one that is robotically taught to us in schools), neurodivergent people have their strengths outside of the box and tend to create entirely new paths for themselves.

Now, as we said before, neurodivergent is a nonmedical term. The same applies to neurotypical people. This means that it's not a condition and that even people who have the same diagnosis may present different signs and symptoms of it from each other. It also means that it's not preventable or "curable," and it shouldn't be, because there is not a single thing wrong with being neurodivergent. Therapy may offer a way to help manage the most overwhelming symptoms, but it will never try to erase them.

With that said, some common traits neurodivergent people may present are a tendency to struggle with soft skills, like emotional intelligence, social interactions, and working in groups; exhibiting physical behaviors that neurotypical people consider "odd," such as standing very close to the people they are interacting with or listening to, speaking too loudly to others even in quiet spaces; performing self-soothing actions such as rocking themselves in public or making irregular hand movements.

Some "common" (everyone is unique) "types" (the categories are blurry at best) of neurodiversity are ADHD, also known as Attention

Deficit Hyperactivity Disorder (ADHD); OCD, or Obsessive-Compulsive Disorder (OCD); and Autism Spectrum Disorder, which can be referred to as just "autism" or "ASD." People with ADHD are individuals who may seem restless, impulsive, and inattentive, as they have trouble being still, thinking before acting, and keeping focused for long periods of time. ADHD is often noticed in childhood, and it can last into adulthood and beyond, but there are also cases of people go their whole lives (or most of them) without ever being diagnosed, always wondering why it is so difficult for them to concentrate, stop daydreaming, misplacing things, staying quiet or interrupting people.

Fidgeting, squirming, not finishing what one started, and taking things that aren't theirs are all well-known traits of people with ADHD.

OCD is a mental health disorder characterized by a pattern of unwanted obsessions, intrusive thoughts and images, and urges that trigger from mildly to extremely distressing emotions (Mayo Clinic, 2020). The obsessive and compulsive behaviors that people with OCD deal with on a daily basis can go from manageable to severe depending on the day and the level of stress the person is in, with more stress equaling more demanding compulsions. However, they are often short-lived and don't interfere with daily lives—not enough to make it unbearable, at least in most cases.

The truth is, repeating compulsions takes a lot of time, and the intrusive thoughts can become really overwhelming and exhausting. People with OCD are aware that they are not realistic—they know that their families won't die if they don't arrange their canned goods with the brand facing forwards, and they understand that they won't contract any incurable disease if they don't wash their hands until they are pink. However, it's almost impossible for them to stop these thoughts, and sometimes giving in is just the less painful option, even if it makes them feel like their obsessions control them.

Autism is a lifelong developmental disability that includes a broad range of conditions characterized by social, behavioral, and speech challenges. People with autism often exhibit repetitive or restricted behaviors, such as lining up objects (their toys, perhaps); repeating words or phrases over and over (which is called echolalia); getting upset by minor changes (like their previously lined up toys being misaligned or picked up); have intense interests (like reciting the equivalent of entire encyclopedias about whales or know everything there is to know about ancient weaving techniques); have unusual reactions to the way things sound, smell, taste, look and feel (they may get overwhelmed or really calmed down by certain noises, not be able to swallow certain food because of their textures or avoid specific types of fabric that they cannot stand) (Jo Rudy, 2022b).

Some people with autism may have advanced conversational skills; meanwhile, others may be nonverbal; some may need a lot of support, while others may live entirely independently. It all depends on which range of the spectrum they are in, going from severely challenging to highly skilled.

Dialectical Behavioral Therapy for Neurodivergent People

Neurodivergent people have brains that have developed or work differently from those of neurotypical people, so their strengths and struggles are vastly different from each other—the way neurodivergent people learn, communicate, and perceive the world around them differs from the norm, and as such, the help they need is also different. What works for most may not have any effect on others, even among people with the same type of neurodivergence. In this case, dialectical behavioral therapy offers a treatment with specialized skills and strategies that are centered specifically on the social and emotional challenges in one's life.

DBT validates the patient's feelings, accepting them without judgment, no matter what they have (or haven't) done. DBT assists its patients as they learn how to regulate their emotions and navigate social situations and motivates them to find new ways to deal with things that will improve their quality of life without forcing them into a mold. Self-control and balance between the logical and the emotional parts of one's mind are two of the main themes of DBT and are considered necessary for the patients to be able to become integrated with their environment, hold themselves accountable for their own actions, find their own paths in life while staying true to themselves, accept their imperfections (which every single person in the world have), and embrace them.

It's important to clarify that dialectical behavioral therapy doesn't encourage patients to be compliant, nor does it stand for an absolute transformation of the self. By creating an environment free of shame, pity, and condemnation, dialectical behavioral therapy aims to provide its patients with the chance to be fully honest about their feelings and behaviors without having to face any form of punishment or chastising because of them. DBT helps clients to come to terms with and find out the reasons behind the ways they think and act with no hard discipline or retribution involved. Once that happens, the DBT therapist is able to create a plan for recovery in which change is driven by the patient, involving them in the process so they may take their lives into their own hands, empowered and supported every step of the way. The fight is against negative, harmful habits, and nothing else.

Mindfulness is an excellent and effective weapon against intrusive thoughts, for example. And there is nothing better than emotional regulation for curving the need to immediately act on one's catastrophic feelings and stop the belief that the worst will happen no matter what one does or says.

Distress tolerance skills will help patients get through times when everything seems overwhelming and stressful, especially when taught and discussed in group sessions, where each person can share their own story and struggles with the rest, helping others realize that they are not alone and that they have never been. Furthermore, interpersonal effectiveness can make neurodivergent people understand that there is no need for them to mask, "camouflage," or imitate neurotypical people in social situations, hiding their neurodivergent traits to fit in with others. The truth is, the people worth having in their life will accept them as they are, and interpersonal effectiveness is a great way to learn that lesson.

What's more, dialectical behavioral therapy focuses on balance, no judgment, and calculated progressive change. This makes it a particularly good approach for autistic people, thanks to its clear structure and concepts. The abilities taught in DBT can also help them to set up care plans suitable to use as interventions during high-stress, overwhelming moments—changing or avoiding certain environments to prevent meltdowns, for example, or, if these seem to be inevitable, establish a solid system to deal with the aftermath, such as eliminating all sensorial stimuli or going to a safe space, turning off all the lights and lying on one's bed belly up, staring at the ceiling while box breathing.

However, as we mentioned at the beginning of the chapter, what works for one person may not for another, but that's what DBT therapists are there for—to help their patients find the best ways to support themselves.

Additionally, being able to train one's social skills and learning how to handle different social situations has been proven particularly good for reducing the vulnerability that autistic patients struggle with in social settings. Practicing their social skills gives them the opportunity to master the art of setting boundaries and recognize possible threats in the manner of the people that approach them. And remember, when a person learns how to improve their own emotional and social life, they are also preventing themselves from developing negative habits such as self-isolation, self-harm, and suicidality.

Dialectical Behavioral Therapy for Anxiety Disorders

Now, though anxiety is not technically a kind of neurodivergence, it can be considered as such. The truth is that both neurodivergent and neurotypical people can have anxiety, though it is a consistent trait in many neurodiversities, like autism and ADHD. But whether or not the medical experts ever reach a consensus, anxiety disorders can also be treated with dialectical behavioral therapy. And that's what we are here for.

See, the extreme feelings of fear, worry, and unease that patients with anxiety disorders face every day can be difficult to cope with and manage, as they don't arise from threats to their lives, health,or well-being. No, for patients with anxiety disorders, those intense emotions just arise, causing even more distress and many problems for the patients. As such, dialectical behavioral therapy can offer them an effective clinical approach that will help them to be in control of their feelings and emotions, working them through the process of acquiring proper coping mechanisms and applying them to their daily lives.

Mindfulness: by teaching them self-awareness and how to be in the present moment, will aid them in their journey to stop worrying both about past events and the unknown future. In the distress tolerance module, for example, the skill of radical acceptance (accepting things as they are, like not being welcomed somewhere or liked by someone, without taking it personally) can guide them through the motions of dealing with panic inducing thoughts and circumstances. This will, in turn, help patients break the cycle of anxiety, which is a process where a person avoids their fears and pushes back their problems, causing them to become increasingly more powerful as time passes. Self-soothing skills may come in handy as well.

As for emotional regulation, it is the same as always; it works in tandem with distress tolerance and helps with overwhelming emotions. Patients with anxiety disorder are taught how to decrease their negative emotions and increase their positive ones, which has a high chance of making them happier, more confident, and more stable.

That said, interpersonal effectiveness skills for anxiety patients focus heavily on teaching them how to say no. See, anxiety patients often lack assertiveness and the ability to speak up for themselves with honesty. They can go their whole lives without even realizing that a major factor in their stress level is just how deep their need to please others run—even at their own expense. By saying yes to everything, they let themselves be taken advantage of, which can only worsen their inability to relax and not panic. And so, a DBT therapist may give their patient everyday situations and make them practice what they would do in each one, so they may be ready for them if they were to happen outside of the therapist's office.

Activities to Help With Anxiety Disorder

Living with anxiety is not easy, but there are many things you can do to help with it quickly and effectively. Writing down the causes of your anxiety, which we discussed in chapter two, is one; journaling (chapter four) and mindfulness meditation (chapter five) are also known for helping greatly. Doing exercise, dancing around and cleaning are amazing options if you feel jittery, and as are taking a hot bath, breathing exercises, and doing yoga if you feel overwhelmed. And even though I would love to add some stress baking recipes for you to try to make, or some knitting patterns that are great for grounding oneself, or some book recommendations that have a particularly effective way to make you feel calm and comfortable in your own skin, I choose instead to recommend this particular activity for your anxiety: walk and talk.

Yes, not a novel idea, I am aware. However, it is incredibly effective. Allow me to tell you how I do it:

- First, I find a place that's big enough and where I can be alone, and I clear it. It may be the garden, where I have to make sure the hose it's properly stored and there is no cat poop laying around, or it may be the dining room, where I tuck the chairs in and often have to put the broom and mop in their rightful places as to not trip over them. Wherever it may be, make sure that you have a place to walk freely in, and something to walk around of. In my case, I drag a plastic chair to the garden and use the actual dining table in the dining room.
- Now, I know that this may sound impossible to do if you live with many people. I'm about to ask you to talk out loud, and

talking out loud while doing laps around a chair has certainly given my neighbors quite a few things to talk about. Don't worry. You can do this laying in your bed and thinking, or out in the street and whispering under your breath. However, I greatly recommend this exact method if you ever find yourself home alone as you are being attacked by your own thoughts, or if you don't mind receiving a few weird stares. It may be useful to know that, in my experience, people get used to it very soon.

- Alright, I warned you before, but now you have to talk. Outloud. You don't have to scream or be too loud, but you should be able to clearly hear yourself talk.
- You are all set! Keep talking, now. Walk and talk and tell the wind about the source or sources of your anxiety. Is it a person, a place, or a situation? Is it something that happened long ago, recently, or that may happen in the future? Is it something you have direct influence over, or something that's entirely out of your control? Be what it may be, lay it out in detail for yourself, and try to find all the reasons why it's worrying you. It doesn't matter if the reasons make no sense, or someone else may consider them dumb. This is your venting session, and the goal is to make you feel better. So try to focus on that, and nothing else.
- Once you have laid out your reasons, try to address them one by one. Is there any way in which you could make it better? Any way in which you can prepare? Maybe you are anxious because you have a job interview soon, and you need the job, and you are worried you may not get it. You could try to rehearse the interview, looking up typical questions and answering one by one in an organized, professional way. You could try to find out more about the company and what they are looking for in their employees, and make sure you meet those requirements. You could take a short course in public speaking (some only take a few hours) to boost your

confidence. You could watch a ted talk or polish your curriculum or manifest yourself getting the job. You have many options! Brainstorm and discuss them with yourself regardless of how silly or difficult or useless they may be. Whether you find an appropriate solution for your problem or not at the end of it all, you will have considered all possible options from all possible points of view. And I can promise you that, whatever the problem is, it will seem much less scary once you have prepared yourself mentally for it.

- That's it! Do this as many times as you need, as often as you need. Remember, the most important part is to get it out in a healthy way. Take all the time and tries you need to do that.

CHAPTER 9
FINDING A THERAPIST

Think of firefighters—think of police officers, paramedics, lifeguards, or first responders of any kind. The people that are first on the scene of an emergency, who are meant to provide aid or conflict resolution in the midst of a disaster. Can you picture it? Well, being a dialectical behavioral therapist is not too different from that. Definitely not for the faint of heart. A DBT therapist must be willing to learn, take on a challenge, and face any problem that the patient may bring into the room; they have to be able to use their training, knowledge, and experience to save a life. It's no easy task, but it is the one that their calling entails.

It's a dialectical behavioral therapist's job to go beyond the therapy room and be in contact with their patients so they can receive assistance as they apply the behaviors that were taught to them in skills training to their day-to-day lives. They need to be available between sessions so they can be reached during times of need; so that their patients can learn how to change the way they handle difficult situations in the moment when it matters.

Of course, a therapist can and is meant to establish how frequently they can be called and how quickly they will call back if they are not available at the exact moment of the call. Therapists are people too, and they have their own lives and limits. Patients should expect them to set an example by implementing healthy boundaries, such as keeping the calls brief and, in some cases, waiting twenty-four hours to contact them again after calling. This last one serves the purpose of ensuring that the patient will not become entirely reliant on their therapist to function and will hopefully make it easier for them to adapt to the use of their newly acquired skills. After all, the role of a dialectical behavioral therapist is to find the correct balance between acceptance and change, and not cross the line between providing support and encouraging codependency. Finding the therapist that better suits your needs may be a challenge in itself, but a hundred percent worth it. Do not give up.

As for who exactly qualifies as a DBT therapist, well—psychiatrists, psychiatric nurses, psychologists, social workers, and family therapists can all be DBT therapists, as long as they have a state-issued certificate and are licensed mental health professionals with experience or knowledge in the patient's area of concern, like eating disorders, BPD or PTSD. Talking with people you trust is a good place to start looking for one, as they may know someone who can refer you to a trustworthy therapist. Overall, what you need is an accepting, patient person, to metaphorically, hold your hand as you take your first steps toward self-healing and recovery.

CONCLUSION

All in all, it's always a good idea to go to therapy. Yes, it may be expensive, and yes, it can take its sweet time, but no amount of self-help books, internet advice, or self-affirmations can ever compensate for being assisted by a professional. If you are ever going to invest in anything, let it be on your own mental health. Investing in your mental health is, after all, investing in your future, and there is nothing quite as beneficial as that. What's more, the long-term effect may take, well, a long time, but you are bound to start feeling better after the first few therapy sessions. After the very first one, even. Therapy has a knack for making people feel like there is hope for the future, like things will get better. And this is the truth.

Be mindful. Take a deep breath as you clutch this book between your hands and realize that here, right now, you have the power to change your life however you like. This is the present moment. There is nothing you can do about the past, so let it go, and there is nothing to fear about the future if you prepare for it.

Regulate your emotions. It is scary. It is too much responsibility. It all may seem overwhelming and impossible and so, so far away… but you ought to understand that it is just your panic talking. Everyone is afraid of what they don't know, but the good thing about the unknown is that, as long as you have a guide and support, it could turn out to be the best thing that ever happened to you. So that sudden anguish you are feeling, that distress? You know what I'm going to say about it, and yet I will say it anyway—tolerate it. Breathe in, hold it for four seconds, and breathe out for four seconds. Wait for another four seconds. Start again. You have gotten through worse, and this? This isn't bad at all.

Talk with your friends, your family, and the strangers on the internet that are with you well every day. Take it to your comfort characters in the media, to your favorite songs and artists, to your most beloved movies and TV shows. To your pet, your plant, your stuffed animal, or the neighborhood cat that you feed on Tuesday mornings. Let it all give you the strength you need to keep going and consider; aren't all of them cheering you on? Wouldn't they all—real, fictional, and inanimate—want you to see yourself thrive, find your path, be at peace, and be happy? Don't you? Think about the child you were, the person you could be. Don't you desire all the good things in the world for them?

You do. You do.

So go ahead. If you ever doubted, if you ever felt scared, if you were ever advised against it, let all that uncertainty melt into the pages of this book, and go look for the help you need to get better and never stop. Now you have a whole arsenal of advice, strategies, and exercises to go with it. You know how it's going to go, what's going to happen. You know what you have to look for and what you can expect. You are ready.

And if no one else does, I believe in you. I believe you will get better. I believe you will achieve your dreams and goals and the happiness you deserve. I may not know you personally, but I know you are reading this book, and since you are reading this book, it means that you have what it takes to make it. You have the interest and the will, and now, you also have the means.

You are on your way to becoming unstoppable. So do. Not. Stop

FREE GIFT

Greetings!

First of all, we want to thank you for reading our books. We aim to create the very best books for our readers.

Now we invite you to join our exclusive list. As a subscriber, you will receive a free gift, weekly tips, free giveaways, discounts and so much more.

<u>All of this is 100% free with no strings attached!</u>

To claim your bonus simply head to the link below or scan the QR code below.

RELOVEPSYCHOLOGY

https://www.subscribepage.com/relovepsychology

REFERENCES

Addict behavior | Most common patterns of substance abuse addiction. (2022, April 25). The Recovery Village Drug and Alcohol Rehab. https://www.therecoveryvillage.com/family-friend-portal/addict-behavior-common-patterns-substance-abuse-addiction/#:~:text=They%20will%20do%20things%20like

ADHD. (n.d.). Kidshealth. https://kidshealth.org/en/parents/adhd.html

American Foundation for Suicide Prevention. (2019, December 25). Risk factors, protective factors, and warning signs. https://afsp.org/risk-factors-protective-factors-and-warning-signs

American Psychiatric Association. (2020, December). What is a substance use Disorder?" www.psychiatry.org/patients-families/addiction-substance-use-disorders/what-is-a-substance-use-disorder

American Psychiatric Association. (2022a, October). What is obsessive-compulsive disorder? https://www.psychiatry.org/patients-families/obsessive-compulsive-disorder/what-is-obsessive-compulsive-disorder

American Psychiatric Association. (2022b, November). What is posttraumatic stress disorder (PTSD)? https://www.psychiatry.org/patients-families/ptsd/what-is-ptsd

Anwar, B. (2022, April 27). DBT for PTSD & trauma. Talkspace. https://www.talkspace.com/mental-health/conditions/dbt-for-ptsd/

Anwar, B. (2022, September 28). DBT for anxiety. Talkspace. https://www.talkspace.com/mental-health/conditions/articles/dbt-for-anxiety/#:~:text=%E2%80%9CDBT%20is%20an%20effective%20therapeutic

Aylward, L. (n.d.). Recovering from meltdowns: Info for autistic people and carers. Bristol Autism Support. https://www.bristolautismsupport.org/recovering-meltdowns-autistic-people-carers/

Beat Eating disorders. (n.d.). Binge eating disorder. https://www.beateatingdisorders.org.uk/get-information-and-support/about-eating-disorders/types/binge-eating-disorder/

Borchard, T. J. (2011, June 28). Marsha Linehan: What is dialectical behavioral therapy (DBT)? Psych Central. https://psychcentral.com/blog/marsha-linehan-what-is-dialectical-behavioral-therapy-dbt#3

BorderlinerNotes. (2017a, April 14). Marsha Linehan - How she came to develop dialectical behavior therapy (DBT)[Video]. YouTube. https://youtu.be/bULL3sSc_-I

BorderlinerNotes. (2017b, April 14). Marsha Linehan - Strategies for emotion regulation [Video]. YouTube. https://youtu.be/lXFYV8L3sHQ

Bothwell, S. (n.d.). DBT dialectical behavioral therapy and eating disorders. Eating Disorder Hope. https://www.eatingdisorderhope.com/treatment-for-eating-disorders/types-of-treatments/dialectical-behavioral-therapy-dbt

Bradley, S. (2021, April 2). The top 7 reasons why people start doing drugs. New Life 360°. https://newlife360inc.com/blog/why-do-people-do-drugs

Buffum Taylor, R. (n.d.). Dialectical behavioral therapy. WebMD. https://www.webmd.com/mental-health/dialectical-behavioral-therapy?fbclid=IwAR2o0-4pjnBZ3SSFt3KUJxOXL2GUHzdb8_U2fmwr1bhCMClxi01INY0gtjI

Carmel, M. (n.d.). Dialectical behavioral therapy in the treatment of binge eating disorder. National Eating Disorders Association. www.nationaleatingdisorders.org/blog/dbt-in-treatment-of-binge-eating-disorder.

Carrico, B. (2021, June 15). Dialectical behavior therapy for anxiety, depression and more. Psych Central. https://psychcentral.com/lib/dialectical-behavior-therapy-for-more-than-borderline-personality-disorder#dbt-for-anxiety

Centers for Disease Control and Prevention (n.d.a). Signs & symptoms. https://www.cdc.gov/ncbddd/autism/signs.html#:~:text=Autism%20spectrum%20disorder%20(ASD)%20is

Centers for Disease Control and Prevention. (n.d.b). What is ASD? https://www.cdc.gov/ncbddd/autism/facts.html

Centers for Disease Control and Prevention. (n.d.c). What is ADHD? https://www.cdc.gov/ncbddd/adhd/facts.html

Chung, M. (2022, April 22). DBT for borderline personality disorder (BPD). Talkspace. https://www.talkspace.com/mental-health/conditions/articles/dbt-for-borderline-personality-disorder/

Cirelli, C. (2022, April 12). Tips for coping with cravings. Mountain Laurel Recovery Center. https://mountainlaurelrecoverycenter.com/coping-cravings-triggers/

Cleveland Clinic. (n.d.a). Borderline personality disorder (BPD): Symptoms, treatment, causes. https://my.clevelandclinic.org/health/diseases/9762-borderline-personality-disorder-bpd

Cleveland Clinic. (n.d.b). Dialectical behavior therapy (DBT). https://my.clevelandclinic.org/health/treatments/22838-dialectical-behavior-therapy-dbt

Cleveland Clinic. (n.d.c). Diuretics. https://my.clevelandclinic.org/health/treatments/21826-diuretics

Cleveland Clinic. (n.d.d). Meditation. https://my.clevelandclinic.org/health/articles/17906-meditation

Cleveland Clinic. (n.d.e). Neurodivergent. https://my.clevelandclinic.org/health/symptoms/23154-neurodivergent

Cleveland Clinic. (n.d.f). Substance use disorder. https://my.clevelandclinic.org/health/diseases/16652-drug-addiction-substance-use-disorder-sud

Cowden, S. (2020, February 18). Dialectical behavioral therapy for eating disorders. Verywell Mind. https://www.verywellmind.com/dialectical-behavior-therapy-for-eating-disorders-1138350

Compitus, K. (2020, October 1). What are distress tolerance skills? The ultimate

DBT toolkit. PositivePsychology. https://positivepsychology.com/distress-tolerance-skills/#:~:text=A%20person%27s%20ability%20to%20manage

Cuncic, A. (2022, August 20). What is "just for today" in NA? Verywell Mind. https://www.verywellmind.com/what-is-just-for-today-in-na-narcotics-anonymous-5649693#:~:text=Just%20for%20Today%20in%20Narcotics,around%20one%20of%20the%20Steps.

DBT for anxiety: How does it work? (2018, November 20). Ranch Creek Recovery. https://ranchcreekrecovery.com/blog/dbt-exercises-anxiety/

DBT consultation team. (n.d.). Behavioral Tech. https://behavioraltech.org/resources/faqs/dbt-consultation-team/

DBT's Approach to treating individuals at high risk for suicide. (2019, September 1). Behavioral Tech. https://behavioraltech.org/dbt-approach-treating-individuals-high-risk-suicide/

DBTSelfHelp. (n.d.a). Daily Cards. https://dbtselfhelp.com/dbt-skills-list/miscellaneous/diary-cards/

DBTSelfHelp. (n.d.b). Wise mind. https://dbtselfhelp.com/dbt-skills-list/mindfulness/wise-mind/#:~:text=DBT%20founder%20Marsha%20Linehan%20describes,something%20in%20a%20centered%20way.%E2%80%9D

Dialectical. (n.d.). Collins Dictionary. https://www.collinsdictionary.com/dictionary/english/dialectical

Dialectical behavioural therapy (n.d.). One Seed Sydney. https://www.oneseedsydney.com/dbt-sydney#:~:text=The%20term%20%22dialectical%22%20comes%20from,results%20than%20either%20one%20alone.

Dialectical behavior therapy for substance use disorders. (2016, July 1). Behavioral Tech. https://behavioraltech.org/dbt-substance-use-disorders/

Dimeff, L. A., & Linehan, M. M. (2008, June). Dialectical behavior therapy for substance abusers. Addiction Science & Clinical Practice, 4(2), 39-47. https://www.ncbi.nlm.nih.gov/pmc/articles/PMC2797106/

Editorial Staff (2022). How can the muscular system be harmed by the effects of drug addiction? American Addiction Centers. https://americanaddictioncenters.org/health-complications-addiction/muscular-system

Embogama. (2016, July 5). Difference between CBT and DBT. Pediaa. https://pediaa.com/difference-between-cbt-and-dbt/

Ertel, A. (2022, September 27). DBT for depression. Talkspace. https://www.talkspace.com/mental-health/conditions/articles/dbt-for-depression/

Estavillo, M. (2020, September 1). The difference between passive and active suicide ideation. Biltmore Psychology and Counseling. https://www.biltmorecounseling.com/anxiety/the-difference-b-n-passive-and-active-suicide-ideation/

Falconberry, K. (2022, August 25). Does dialectical behavioral therapy (BDT) work for anxiety. Lifeskills South Florida. https://www.lifeskillssouthflorida.com/mental-health-blog/does-dialectical-behavioral-therapy-dbt-work-for-anxiety/

Greene, P. (2020, June 3). Your easy guide to DBT's TIPP skills. Manhattan Center for Cognitive Behavioral Therapy. https://www.manhattancbt.com/archives/1452/dbt-tipp-skills/

Guarda, A. (2021, March). What are eating disorders? https://www.psychiatry.org/patients-families/eating-disorders/what-are-eating-disorders

Guarnotta, E. (2022, December 16). Types of BPD: Signs, symptoms & when to get help. Choosing Therapy. https://www.choosingtherapy.com/types-of-bpd/

Hazelden Betty Ford Foundation. (2019, March 20). The twelve steps of alcoholic anonymous. https://www.hazeldenbettyford.org/articles/twelve-steps-of-alcoholics-anonymous

Harmer, B., Lee, S., Duong, T. V. H., & Saadabadi, A. (2022). Suicidal ideation. StatPearls Publishing. https://pubmed.ncbi.nlm.nih.gov/33351435/

Healthdirect Australia. (2020, May 6). Dialectical behavior therapy (DBT). https://www.healthdirect.gov.au/dialectical-behaviour-therapy-dbt.

Is anxiety neurodivergent? What does the science say? (2021, February 16). XanFree. https://xanfree.com/blogs/research-resources/is-anxiety-neurodivergent-what-does-the-science-say

John Hopkins Medicine. (n.d.). Bulimia nervosa. https://www.hopkinsmedicine.org/health/conditions-and-diseases/eating-disorders/bulimia-nervosa

Khat, K. (n.d.). Drug paraphernalia. Fast Facts. https://www.justice.gov/archive/ndic/pubs6/6445/6445p.pdf

Ladysnessa. (2019, August 23). Dialectical behavioral therapy & autism: An empowering set of skills. NeuroClastic. https://neuroclastic.com/dialectical-behavioral-therapy-autism-an-empowering-set-of-skills/

Lebow, H. I. (2022, July 27). Is anxiety neurodivergent? What the research says. Psych Central. https://psychcentral.com/anxiety/is-anxiety-neurodivergent#is-anxiety-neurodivergent

Leonard, J. (2020, June 24). Everything to know about dialectical behavioral therapy. MedicalNewsToday. https://www.medicalnewstoday.com/articles/everything-to-know-about-dialectical-behavioral-therapy

Linardon, J. (2020, March 28). Applying dialectical behavior therapy to eating disorders. Break Binge Eating. https://breakbingeeating.com/dialectical-behavior-therapy/

Linehan, M. (2020). Living a life worth living: A memoir. Random House.

Linehan, M. M., & Wilks, C. R. (2015). The course and evolution of dialectical behavior therapy. American Journal of Psychotherapy, 69(2), 97–110. https://doi.org/10.1176/appi.psychotherapy.2015.69.2.97

Linehan, M., Reitz, R. O. (n.d.). Using dialectical behavioral therapy to treat suicidality and self-harm. Goop. https://goop.com/wellness/health/dialectical-behavioral-therapy/

LOiva. (2022, June 10). 10 benefits of meditation. CanoHealth. https://canohealth.com/news/blog/10-benefits-of-meditation/

Jo Rudy, L. (2022a, August 27). What does "neurotypical" mean? Verywell Health. https://www.verywellhealth.com/what-does-it-mean-to-be-neurotypical-260047

Jo Rudy, L. (2022b, February 14). Repetitive behaviors in autism. Verywell Health. https://www.verywellhealth.com/repetitive-behaviors-in-autism-260582#:~:text=Repetitive%2C%20purposeless%20behaviors%20are%20a,thing%20over%20and%20over%20again.

Mairanz, A. (2019, December 6). How to practice interpersonal effectiveness every day. Empower Your Mind Therapy. https://eymtherapy.com/blog/practice-interpersonal-effectiveness-dbt-skill/

Mayer Robinson, K. (2017). How journaling helps manage depression. WebMD. https://www.webmd.com/depression/features/writing-your-way-out-of-depression

May, M. M., Richardi, T. M., & Barth, K. S. (2016). Dialectical behavior therapy as treatment for borderline personality disorder. Mental Health Clinician, 6(2), 62-67. https://doi.org/10.9740/mhc.2016.03.62

Mayo Clinic. (2018a, February 20). Anorexia nervosa. https://www.mayoclinic.org/diseases-conditions/anorexia-nervosa/symptoms-causes/syc-20353591

Mayo Clinic. (2018b, May 5). Binge-eating disorders. https://www.mayoclinic.org/diseases-conditions/binge-eating-disorder/symptoms-causes/syc-20353627

Mayo Clinic. (2018c, May 10). Bulimia nervosa. https://www.mayoclinic.org/diseases-conditions/bulimia/symptoms-causes/syc-20353615

Mayo Clinic. (2019a). Mental illness. https://www.mayoclinic.org/diseases-conditions/mental-illness/symptoms-causes/syc-20374968#:~:text=Certain%20factors%20may%20increase%20your

Mayo Clinic. (2019b, July 17). Borderline personality disorder. https://www.mayoclinic.org/diseases-conditions/borderline-personality-disorder/symptoms-causes/syc-20370237

Mayo Clinic. (2020). Obsessive-compulsive disorder (OCD). https://www.mayoclinic.org/diseases-conditions/obsessive-compulsive-disorder/symptoms-causes/syc-20354432

Mayo Clinic. (2o22a, April 29). Meditation: A simple, fast way to reduce stress. https://www.mayoclinic.org/tests-procedures/meditation/in-depth/meditation/art-20045858

Mayo Clinic. (2022b, October 4). Drug addiction (substance use disorder). https://www.mayoclinic.org/diseases-conditions/drug-addiction/symptoms-causes/syc-20365112

Mayo Clinic. (2022c, October 14). Depression (Major depressive disorder). https://www.mayoclinic.org/diseases-conditions/depression/symptoms-causes/syc-20356007

Mayo Clinic. (2022d, December 13). Post-traumatic Stress Disorder (PTSD). https://www.mayoclinic.org/diseases-conditions/post-traumatic-stress-disorder/symptoms-causes/syc-20355967

McAdam, E. (2021, October 14). How to journal for depression and anxiety: 6 ways to process emotions with writing. Therapy In A Nutshell. https://therapyinanutshell.com/how-to-journal-for-anxiety-and-depression-6-ways-to-process-emotions-with-writing/

McCallum Place Eating Disorder Center. (2023). Eating Disorder Risk Factors. https://www.mccallumplace.com/eating-disorder/risk-factors-stats/#:~:text=Weight%20Concerns%2C%20Dieting%2C%20and%20Negative,factors%20for%20developing%20eating%20disorders.

Miller, W. R., Meyers, R. J., & Hiller-Sturmhöfel, S. (1999). The community-reinforcement approach. Alcohol Research & Health, 23 (2), 116-121. https://www.ncbi.nlm.nih.gov/pmc/articles/PMC6760430/

Mind. (n.d.a). Obsessive-compulsive disorder (OCD). https://www.mind.org.uk/information-support/types-of-mental-health-problems/obsessive-compulsive-disorder-ocd/about-ocd/

Mind. (n.d.b). Dialectical behaviour therapy (DBT). https://www.mind.org.uk/information-support/drugs-and-treatments/talking-therapy-and-counselling/dialectical-behaviour-therapy-dbt/

Moore, M. (2022, July 7). 4 DBT skills for everyday challenges. Psych Central. https://psychcentral.com/health/dbt-skills-therapy-techniques#distress-tolerance

National Autistic Society. (n.d.). What is autism? https://www.autism.org.uk/advice-and-guidance/what-is-autism

National Institute of Drug Abuse. (2020, July). Addiction and health. https://nida.nih.gov/publications/drugs-brains-behavior-science-addiction/addiction-health

National Institute of Mental Health. (2017). Borderline personality disorder. www.nimh.nih.gov/health/topics/borderline-personality-disorder.

National Institute of Mental Health. (n.d.a). Borderline personality disorder. https://www.nimh.nih.gov/health/topics/borderline-personality-disorder

National Institute of Mental Health. (n.d.b). Post Traumatic stress disorder. https://www.nimh.nih.gov/health/topics/post-traumatic-stress-disorder-ptsd

National Institute of Mental Health. (n.d.c). Substance use and co-occurring mental disorders. https://www.nimh.nih.gov/health/topics/substance-use-and-mental-health#:~:text=A%20substance%20use%20disorder%20

National Library of Medicine. (n.d.). Post-traumatic stress disorder. https://medlineplus.gov/posttraumaticstressdisorder.html

NHS. (n.d.). Attention deficit hyperactivity disorder (ADHD). https://www.nhs.uk/conditions/attention-deficit-hyperactivity-disorder-adhd/

NSW Health. (2004). Framework for suicide risk assessment and management. https://www.health.nsw.gov.au/mentalhealth/resources/Publications/suicide-risk.pdf

Optimum Performance Institute. (n.d.). The four types of borderline personality disorder. https://www.optimumperformanceinstitute.com/bpd-treatment/bpd-symptoms-examined/

Pederson, L. (2020, May 5). How to help someone with OCD. Mental Health Systems. https://www.mhs-dbt.com/blog/help-ocd-with-dbt/#:~:text=How%20Does%20DBT%20Help%20OCD

Posttraumatic stress disorder (PTDS) in children. (n.d.) Stanford Medicine Children's Health. https://www.stanfordchildrens.org/en/topic/default?id=post-traumatic-stress-disorder-in-children-90-P02579#:~:text=A%20child%20with%20PTSD%20has,may%20have%20nightmares%20or%20flashbacks.

Purse, M. (2019). What is suicidal ideation? Verywell Mind. https://www.verywellmind.com/suicidal-ideation-380609

Ramsay, R. J. (2018, April 30). DBT: The emotional control therapy you need now. ADDitude. https://www.additudemag.com/dbt-for-adhd-dialectical-behavioral-therapy/

Raymond, A. (n.d.). 6 body image activities for eating disorders. Courage to Nourish. https://couragetonourish.com/body-image-activities-for-eating-disorders/

Raypole, C. (2019a, January 25). DBT: Dialectical behavioral therapy skills, techniques, what it treats. Healthline. https://www.healthline.com/health/dbt#techniques

Raypole, C. (2019b, May 24). 30 grounding techniques to quiet distressing thoughts. Healthline. https://www.healthline.com/health/grounding-techniques

Resnick, A. (2021, October 6). What is neurodivergence and what does it mean to be neurodivergent? Verywell Mind. https://www.verywellmind.com/what-is-neurodivergence-and-what-does-it-mean-to-be-neurodivergent-5196627

Rosenblatt, K. (2021, June 21). The 4 types of borderline personality disorder. Talkspace. https://www.talkspace.com/mental-health/conditions/borderline-personality-disorder/types/

Safer, D. L., Telch, C. F., & Agras, W. S. (2001). Dialectical behavior therapy for bulimia nervosa. American Journal of Psychiatry, 158(4), 632-634. https://doi.org/10.1176/appi.ajp.158.4.632

Salters-Pedneault, K. (2021, February 21). How can dialectical behavior therapy for BPD help you? Verywell Mind. https://www.verywellmind.com/dialectical-behavior-therapy-dbt-for-bpd-425454

Sapusek, T. (2014, December 9). Dialectical behavior therapy for depression treatment. Clearview Treatment Programs. https://www.clearviewtreatment.com/resources/blog/dbt-depression-treatment/

Schimelpfening, N. (2022, July 22). What to know about dialectical behavior therapy. Verywell Mind. https://www.verywellmind.com/dialectical-behavior-therapy-1067402

Schwartz, A. (n.d.). Dialectical behavior therapy: What is a dialectic? MentalHelp. https://www.mentalhelp.net/blogs/dialectical-behavior-therapy-what-is-a-dialectic/

SMART Recovery. (2017, January 31). 5 ways to deal with urges and cravings. https://www.smartrecovery.org/5-ways-to-deal-with-urges-and-cravings/

Smith, M., Segal, J. (2022, December 15). Borderline personality disorder (BPD). HelpGuide. https://www.helpguide.org/articles/mental-disorders/borderline-personality-disorder.htm

Stanley, B., Brodsky, B., Nelson, J. D., & Dulit, R. (2007). Brief dialectical behavior therapy (DBT-B) for suicidal behavior and non-suicidal self injury. Archives of Suicide Research, 11(4), 337-341. https://www.tandfonline.com/doi/abs/10.1080/13811110701542069

Steil, R., et al. (2021, November 18). How to treat childhood sexual abuse related PTSD accompanied by risky sexual behavior: A case study on the use of dialectical behavior therapy for posttraumatic stress disorder (DBT-PTSD). Journal of Child & Adolescent Trauma. https://link.springer.com/article/10.1007/s40653-021-00421-6

Stiglmayr, C., et al. (2014, December 18). Effectiveness of dialectic behavioral therapy in routine outpatient care: The Berlin borderline study. Borderline Personality Disorder and Emotion Dysregulation, 1(1), 20. https://pubmed.ncbi.nlm.nih.gov/26401303/

Tartakovsky, M. (2016, September 4). 5 ways to process your emotions through writing. Psych Central. https://psychcentral.com/blog/everyday-creativity/2016/09/5-ways-to-process-your-emotions-through-writing#1

Tackett, B. (2023, January 19). Refusing to give in: 8 ways to beat cravings. American Addiction Centers. https://drugabuse.com/blog/beat-cravings/

The DBT 4 modules: The fundamentals of dialectical behavior therapy. (2022, February 2). Elliott Counseling Group. https://elliottcounselinggroup.com/dbt-four-modules/

The four types of borderline personality disorder (BPD). (2021, January 20). Socal Empowered. https://socalempowered.com/the-four-types-of-borderline-personality-disorder-bpd/

TherapistAid. (2015). The Wise Mind. https://www.therapistaid.com/worksheets/wise-mind

Torres, F. (2020, October). What is depression? American Psychiatric Association. https://www.psychiatry.org/patients-families/depression/what-is-depression

Tull, M. (2022, November 23). How dialectical behavior therapy (DBT) can help people with PTSD. Verywell Mind. https://www.verywellmind.com/dbt-for-ptsd-2797652

Vaughn, S. (2022, November 30). History of dialectical behavior therapy: A very brief introduction. Psychotherapy Academy. https://psychotherapyacademy.org/dbt/history-of-dialectical-behavioral-therapy-a-very-brief-introduction/#:~:text=DBT%20was%20originally%20founded%20in

Vaughn, S. (2022, November 30). The DBT hierarchy: Prioritizing treatment targets. Psychotherapy Academy. https://psychotherapyacademy.org/dbt/prioritizing-targets-the-dbt-hierarchy/

Walker, L. (2018, November 23). What is addiction? DrugAbuse. https://drugabuse.com/addiction/

What is a substance use disorder? (2020, December). American Psychiatric Association. https://www.psychiatry.org/patients-families/addiction-substance-use-disorders/what-is-a-substance-use-disorder

What is Dialectical Behavior Therapy (DBT)? (n.d.). Behavioral Tech. https://behavioraltech.org/resources/faqs/dialectical-behavior-therapy-dbt/

What is it really like to be neurodivergent? (2023, January 05). Zurich. https://www.zurich.com/en/media/magazine/2022/its-all-in-the-mind-what-does-it-mean-to-be-neurodivergent#:~:text=Neurodivergent%20is%20a%20non%2Dmedical,us%20in%20a%20unique%20way.

Who invented DBT? (2020, September 28). Suzanne Wallach. https://suzannewallach.com/blog/who-invented-dbt/

Whyte, A. (2021, October 29). DBT the gold standard for treating adolescent self-harm and suicidal ideation. Evolve Treatment Centers. https://evolvetreatment.com/blog/dbt-teen-self-harm-suicide/

Wikipedia Contributors. (2019, June 16). Dialectical behavior therapy. Wikimedia Foundation. https://en.wikipedia.org/wiki/Dialectical_behavior_therapy

Wise Miller, E. (2015, May 29). 6 steps to mindfulness meditation. Livehappy. https://www.livehappy.com/practice/6-steps-to-mindfulness-meditation

Wisniewski, L., & Ben-Porath, D. D. (2015). Dialectical behavior therapy and eating disorders: The use of contingency management procedures to manage dialectical dilemmas. American Journal of Psychotherapy, 69(2), 129-140. https://doi.org/10.1176/appi.psychotherapy.2015.69.2.129

Zen mindfulness in DBT. (2019, March 11). Behavioral Tech. https://behavioraltech.org/zen-mindfulness-in-dbt/

OTHER BOOKS BY
RELOVE PSYCHOLOGY

Available now in Ebook, Paperback and Hardcover in all regions.

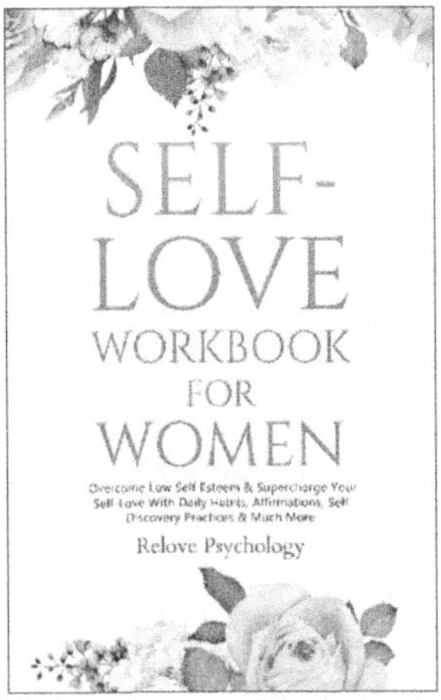

DBT WORKBOOK FOR ADULTS

We sincerely hope you enjoyed our new book ***"DBT Workbook for Adults"***. We would greatly appreciate your feedback with an honest review at the place of purchase.

First and foremost, we are always looking to grow and improve as a team. It is reassuring to hear what works, as well as receive constructive feedback on what should improve. Second, starting out as an unknown author is exceedingly difficult, and Amazon reviews go a long way toward making the journey out of anonymity possible. Please take a few minutes to write an honest review.

Best regards,
Relove Psychology
http://relovepsychology.com

Made in the USA
Monee, IL
24 April 2023

32365772R10066